PARENT-TEACHER COLLECTION

WELCOME!

On behalf of Splash! Publications, we would like to welcome you to *The Thirteen Original Colonies*, one of several books in our American History series. Since this curriculum was designed by teachers, we are positive that you will find it to be the most comprehensive program you have ever utilized to teach students about the thirteen original colonies. We would like to take a few moments to familiarize you with the program.

THE FORMAT

The Thirteen Original Colonies is a 13 lesson program. Our goal is a curriculum that you can use the very first day you purchase our materials. No lessons to plan, comprehension questions to write, activities to create, or vocabulary words to define. Simply open the book and start teaching.

Each of the 13 lessons requires students to complete vocabulary cards, read about one of the thirteen original colonies, and complete a comprehension activity that will expose them to various standardized test formats. In addition, each lesson includes a balanced mix of lower and higher level activities for students to complete. Vocabulary and mapping quizzes, mapping activities teaching reference points and cardinal directions, grid math, research projects utilizing graphic organizers and primary and secondary sources, time lines, and following directions are the types of activities that will guide students through their journey of *The Thirteen Original Colonies*.

THE LESSON PLANS

On the next several pages, you will find the Lesson Plans for *The Thirteen Original Colonies*. The Lesson Plans clearly outline what students must do before, during, and after each lesson. Page numbers are listed so that you will immediately know what you need to photocopy before beginning each lesson. The answers to all activities, quizzes, and comprehension questions are located on pages 94-99.

NOTE: Students will complete a culminating activity at the end of the curriculum. We suggest that students keep the information from each lesson in a notebook or folder.

THE VOCABULARY

Each lesson features words in bold type. We have included a Glossary on pages 88-93 to help students pronounce and define the words. Unlike a dictionary, the definitions in the Glossary are concise and written in context. Remember, we're teachers! Students will be exposed to these vocabulary words in the comprehension activities. They will also be tested on the vocabulary words five times throughout their study of *The Thirteen Original Colonies*.

Students will be responsible for filling out and studying the vocabulary cards. You may want to have students bring in a small box for storing their vocabulary cards. We don't have to tell you that incorporating these words into your Reading an[d Spelling] programs will save time and make the words more meaningful for students.

The Thirteen Original Colonies © 2009
splashpublications.com

Illustrations and cover design by Victoria J. Smith

ISBN 978-1-935255-02-4

OUR OTHER TITLES

COMPLETE STATE HISTORY PROGRAMS

Do American History!
Do Arizona!
Do California!
Do Colorado!
Do Nevada!
Do New Mexico!
Do Texas!
Do Washington!

AMERICAN HISTORY SERIES

New World Explorers
Spanish Explorers & Conquistadors
Early American Government
The American Revolution
Slavery in America
The Civil War
Westward Expansion

STATE HISTORY SERIES

Arizona Geography
Arizona Animals
Arizona History
Arizona Government & Economy
California Geography
California Animals
California History
California Government & Economy
Florida Geography
Florida Animals
Florida History
Florida Government & Economy
Texas Geography
Texas Animals
Texas History
Texas Government & Economy

LITERATURE STUDY GUIDES

Charlotte's Web
Cricket in Times Square
Enormous Egg
Sarah, Plain and Tall

U.S. REGION SERIES

The New England States
The Middle Atlantic States
The Great Lakes States
The Great Plains States
The Southeast States
The Southwest States
The Mountain States
The Pacific States

TABLE OF CONTENTS

THE THIRTEEN ORIGINAL COLONIES

★ TABLE OF CONTENTS

THE THIRTEEN ORIGINAL COLONIES (CONTINUED)

LESSONS *at a* GLANCE

1. Before reading Virginia, students will:
- complete Vocabulary Cards for *Africa, appointed, assault, captives, climate, coast, colonies, confederacy, conflict, cultivate, debt, defeated, dominion, England, fertile, fungus, governor, harvested, historians, indigo, inhabited, indentured servants, loyal, merchants, militia, New World, plantations, prosper, rebellion, representatives, revolted, threatened, wigwam.* (*pg. 1*)

After reading Virginia (*pps. 2-5*), students will:
- answer Virginia Reading Comprehension Questions. (*pg. 6*)
- plot Virginia on the Thirteen Original Colonies Study Guide Map. (*pg. 7*)
- take a Vocabulary Quiz for the Thirteen Original Colonies Part I. (*pps. 8-9*)

2. Before reading Massachusetts, students will:
- complete Vocabulary Cards for *bay, Church of England, European, founded, harbors, kidnapped, official, Pilgrims, Puritan, trampled, treaty.* (*pg. 1*)

After reading Massachusetts (*pps. 10-12*), students will:
- answer Massachusetts Reading Comprehension Questions. (*pg. 13*)
- plot Massachusetts on the Thirteen Original Colonies Study Guide Map. (*pg. 7*)
- use a system of number and letter pairs to complete Grid Math. (*pps. 14-16*)

3. Before reading New Hampshire, students will:
- complete Vocabulary Cards for *allies, Asia, boundaries, council, destructive, determination, encouraged, expanding, expedition, formations, French, granite, interior, keelboats, livestock, production, province, raided, scalps, Scotland, seacoast, shoreline.* (*pg. 1*)

After reading New Hampshire (*pps. 17-20*), students will:
- answer New Hampshire Reading Comprehension Questions. (*pg. 21*)
- plot New Hampshire on the Thirteen Original Colonies Study Guide Map. (*pg. 7*)
- take a Vocabulary Quiz for the Thirteen Original Colonies Part II. (*pps. 22-23*)

★ LESSONS *at a* GLANCE ★

4. Before reading New York, students will:
- complete Vocabulary Cards for *Christians, Dutch, empire, Great Lakes, Greenland, gristmills, incisor, longhouse, North America, North Pole, orchards, preserved, profit, resources, rodent, sawmills, seaport, strait, voyages.* *(pg. 1)*

After reading New York *(pps. 24-27)*, students will:
- answer New York Reading Comprehension Questions. *(pg. 28)*
- plot New York on the Thirteen Original Colonies Study Guide Map. *(pg. 7)*
- follow written directions to draw a beaver. *(pps. 29-30)*

5. Before reading Maryland, students will:
- complete Vocabulary Cards for *admired, autobiography, biographies, Catholics, charter, Protestants, quarreling, Revolutionary War, statute, turmoil.* *(pg. 1)*

After reading Maryland *(pps. 31-32)*, students will:
- answer Maryland Reading Comprehension Questions. *(pg. 33)*
- plot Maryland on the Thirteen Original Colonies Study Guide Map. *(pg. 7)*
- differentiate between primary and secondary sources. *(pg. 34)*
- take a Vocabulary Quiz for the Thirteen Original Colonies Part III. *(pps. 35-36)*

6. Before reading Connecticut, students will:
- complete Vocabulary Cards for *accused, adopted, Bermuda, constitution, elections, independent, overthrown, united, wampum.* *(pg. 1)*

After reading Connecticut *(pps. 37-39)*, students will:
- answer Connecticut Reading Comprehension Questions. *(pg. 40)*
- plot Connecticut on the Thirteen Original Colonies Study Guide Map. *(pg. 7)*
- create a time line for Connecticut's history in Time Travel Part I. *(pg. 41)*
- create a personal time line in Time Travel Part II. *(pg. 42)*

★ LESSONS *at a* GLANCE ★

7.   Before reading Rhode Island, students will:
- complete Vocabulary Cards for *nationalities, Quaker, synagogues.* *(pg. 1)*

After reading Rhode Island *(pps. 43-45)*, students will:
- answer Rhode Island Reading Comprehension Questions. *(pg. 46)*
- plot Rhode Island on the Thirteen Original Colonies Study Guide Map. *(pg. 7)*
- use primary and secondary sources to create the game Find the Fib. *(pps. 47-49)*
  NOTE: You will need to make four copies of page 48 or 49 for each student.

8.   Before reading Delaware, students will:
- complete Vocabulary Cards for *pioneers, pirate, pledged, seized.* *(pg. 1)*

After reading Delaware *(pps. 50-51)*, students will:
- answer Delaware Reading Comprehension Questions. *(pg. 52)*
- plot Delaware on the Thirteen Original Colonies Study Guide Map. *(pg. 7)*
- follow written directions to make a miniature Swedish log cabin. *(pps. 53-55)*

9.   Before reading Pennsylvania, students will:
- complete Vocabulary Cards for *annual, artifacts, Civil War, commandment, exhibits, meadows, motto, species.* *(pg. 1)*

After reading Pennsylvania *(pps. 56-57)*, students will:
- answer Pennsylvania Reading Comprehension Questions. *(pg. 58)*
- plot Pennsylvania on the Thirteen Original Colonies Study Guide Map. *(pg. 7)*
- use cardinal and intermediate directions to plot points of interest on a Pennsylvania map. *(pps. 59-63)*

10.   Before reading North Carolina, students will:
- complete Vocabulary Cards for *ceremonial, extinct, Ireland, knight, military, mound builders, prehistoric, proprietors, reefs, sandbars, Spain.* *(pg. 1)*

After reading North Carolina *(pps. 64-66)*, students will:
- answer North Carolina Reading Comprehension Questions. *(pg. 67)*
- plot North Carolina on the Thirteen Original Colonies Study Guide Map. *(pg. 7)*
- take a Vocabulary Quiz for the Thirteen Original Colonies Part IV. *(pps. 68-69)*

★ LESSONS *at a* GLANCE ★

11. Before reading New Jersey, students will:
  • complete Vocabulary Cards for *epidemic, estates, fertilizer, immigrants, influenza, insisted, Italian, mammoths, measles, smallpox.* *(pg. 1)*

After reading New Jersey *(pps. 70-71)*, students will:
  • answer New Jersey Reading Comprehension Questions. *(pg. 72)*
  • plot New Jersey on the Thirteen Original Colonies Study Guide Map. *(pg. 7)*
  • create a time line for New Jersey's history in Time Travel Part I. *(pg. 73)*
  • create a time line for someone else in Time Travel Part II. *(pg. 74)*

12. Before reading South Carolina, students will:
  • complete Vocabulary Cards for *emblem, palmetto, West Indies.* *(pg. 1)*

After reading South Carolina *(pps. 75-77)*, students will:
  • answer South Carolina Reading Comprehension Questions. *(pg. 78)*
  • plot South Carolina on the Thirteen Original Colonies Study Guide Map. *(pg. 7)*
  • research a famous colonist to complete K•W•L•H chart. *(pps. 79-81)*
  • use K•W•L•H chart to answer famous colonist discussion questions. *(pg. 82)*

13. Before reading Georgia, students will:
  • complete Vocabulary Cards for *legislature, malaria, retained.* *(pg. 1)*

After reading Georgia *(pps. 83-84)*, students will:
  • answer Georgia Reading Comprehension Questions. *(pg. 85)*
  • plot and color code the thirteen original colonies on a map. *(pg. 86)*
  • take a Vocabulary Quiz for the Thirteen Original Colonies Part V. *(pg. 87)*

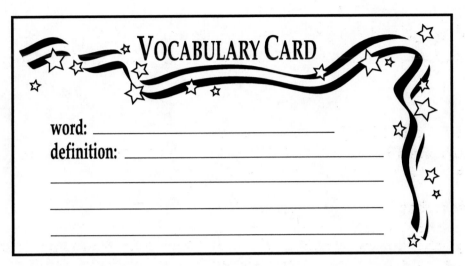

VOCABULARY CARD

word: _____

definition: _____

_____

_____

_____

VOCABULARY CARD

word: _____

definition: _____

_____

_____

_____

VOCABULARY CARD

word: _____

definition: _____

_____

_____

_____

VIRGINIA

Virginia, one of the five Southern **colonies**, was the first of the thirteen original colonies in America. Virginia's nickname is the Old **Dominion** State. It is also known as the Mother of Presidents. Four of the first five presidents of the United States were born in Virginia.

THE JAMESTOWN COLONY

Virginia was not England's first choice for establishing a colony in America. Beginning in 1585, two groups of colonists were sent to Roanoke (ROW•an•oke) Island, near the **coast** of present-day North Carolina. Both colonies failed. In fact, the second group of colonists at Roanoke Island disappeared. What happened to them is still a mystery to this day. Roanoke became known as the famous "Lost Colony."

In 1600, **England** was ready to try again. A group of wealthy **merchants** from London believed that they could make a lot of money in America. The businessmen formed the Virginia Company of London. They offered to pay the way of anyone who wanted to go to America.

To repay the merchants, the colonists had to give the Virginia Company part of any gold or silver found in the **New World**. The colonists were also told to **cultivate** mulberry trees so they could raise silkworms and trade silk with England. The wealthy merchants hired 27 year old John Smith to run the new colony.

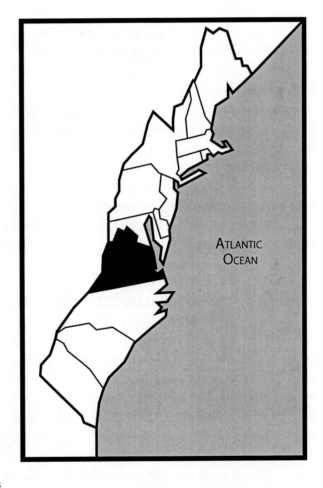

ATLANTIC OCEAN

In 1607, John Smith and a group of more than 100 men and boys landed near the Chesapeake Bay in present-day Virginia. In honor of England's King James I, they named their colony Jamestown.

THE POWHATAN CONFEDERACY

John Smith found that Jamestown was already **inhabited** by Native Americans. The Woodland people, led by Chief Powhatan, were part of the Powhatan **Confederacy**.

The Powhatan Confederacy included at least 30 tribes that spoke the Algonquian (al•GONG•kee•in) language. These tribes lived in **wigwam** villages near the coast. John Smith wrote that there were about 100 families in each village. Each village was led by a chief. In the beginning, the Jamestown colonists had a difficult time surviving and getting along with the Native Americans.

The colonists were unable to find gold. A **fungus** destroyed the mulberry trees. All of the silkworms died. The colonists did not know how to hunt, where to fish, or how to make the water pure so they could drink it. They were also unable to protect themselves from disease-carrying mosquitoes. They were constantly at war with the Native Americans.

In 1608, a supply ship arrived from England. Less than 50 settlers were still alive. In 1609, John Smith was badly injured in a gunpowder explosion. He left Virginia and returned to England for medical care.

CHIEF POWHATAN

THE FIRST GOVERNMENT IN AMERICA

In 1614, Jamestown colonist John Rolfe married the daughter of Chief Powhatan. Her name was Pocahontas. The marriage brought some peace between the Jamestown settlers and the Native Americans. The Native Americans taught the settlers how to grow tobacco. By 1619, things had changed for the colonists. Sir Thomas Dale and Sir George Yeardley were chosen to lead the colony. The Jamestown Colony began to **prosper**.

The Virginia Company was pleased with the positive changes in the colony. Women were sent to Jamestown to marry the men. Each settler was given a piece of land on which to grow tobacco. The colonists elected **representatives** and began making laws for the colony. This group of lawmakers was known as the House of Burgesses (BUR•jis•iz). It was the first type of government formed in the New World.

INDENTURED SERVANTS AND SLAVERY

In 1619, the first black men and women from **Africa** arrived in Jamestown. They had been captured in Africa by Spanish slave traders. On the way to America, Dutch pirates attacked the Spanish ships and stole the Africans. The Dutch pirates sold their black **captives** to the Jamestown colonists as **indentured servants**.

Indentured servants were different from slaves. Slaves were purchased and worked without pay. They remained the property of their owners, or masters, for their entire lives. Indentured servants also worked without pay. After their **debt** was paid, the indentured servants were set free.

Some of Jamestown's black indentured servants earned money by doing extra jobs for their masters or neighbors. After they were set free, they bought property in Virginia. The white colonists treated the black settlers badly. Free blacks had no rights in Jamestown or any of the other colonies. They could not vote. They were not welcome in the same churches and businesses as the white colonists. Virginia's House of Burgesses wrote a law that allowed colonists to own slaves. There were very few free black people in Virginia after that law was written.

THE FIRST NATIVE AMERICAN WAR

In 1624, England took control of Jamestown. Jamestown became a royal colony. A **governor** was chosen by the king of England. Chief Powhatan and his daughter Pocahontas had died. The new chief of the Powhatan Confederacy hated the English colonists. He secretly planned to destroy their settlements in America. The new chief led an **assault** on the Jamestown Colony. More than 300 colonists were killed. This was the first major **conflict** in the New World between the English colonists and the Native Americans. It was during one of these attacks that **historians** believe John Rolfe was probably killed.

The survivors of the battle planned to strike back at the Native Americans. They waited until the fall of the year when all of the crops were ready to be **harvested**. The colonists attacked the Native Americans and destroyed their crops of corn. The Native Americans who survived the attack were left to starve. For the next 12 years, the Jamestown colonists and Native Americans fought for control of Virginia.

In 1634, the Powhatan Confederacy and English colonists made peace. Ten years later, the Native Americans attacked again. During this attack, 300 colonists were killed. Finally, after a two day battle, the Powhatan Confederacy was **defeated**.

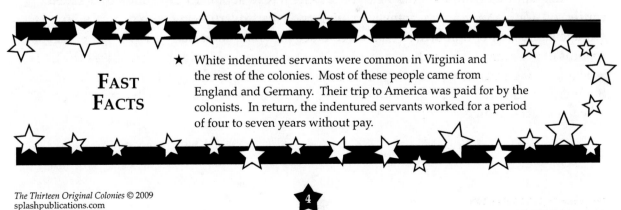

FAST FACTS

★ White indentured servants were common in Virginia and the rest of the colonies. Most of these people came from England and Germany. Their trip to America was paid for by the colonists. In return, the indentured servants worked for a period of four to seven years without pay.

GOVERNOR BERKELEY

In 1660, Charles II became the king of England. He **appointed** Sir William Berkeley as the governor of Virginia. King Charles II demanded that the colonists trade only with England. He felt that this would keep the colonists **loyal** to England.

Governor Berkeley refused to allow the colonists to elect new representatives to the House of Burgesses. Berkeley also kept the colonists from organizing a **militia** to fight against the Native Americans who **threatened** to attack again.

In 1676, the colonists **revolted** against King Charles II and Governor Berkeley. The Jamestown colonists chose Nathaniel Bacon to be their leader.

BACON'S REBELLION

Nathaniel Bacon led the colonists into battle against the Native Americans. After a quick defeat, Bacon and his followers tried to make Governor Berkeley change the way he treated the colonists. The governor refused.

In what became known as Bacon's **Rebellion**, Nathaniel Bacon and his army burned Jamestown to the ground.

The colonists began rebuilding Jamestown. They chose Nathaniel Bacon as their governor. Unfortunately, Bacon became very ill. He died the following year. England selected a new governor for the colony. Like Berkeley, this governor was not well liked by the colonists.

NATHANIEL BACON

THE ECONOMY OF THE SOUTHERN COLONIES

Like the other Southern colonies you will soon read about, Virginia offered its settlers **fertile** soil, forests full of trees, animals to hunt, and rivers overflowing with fish. A warm **climate** and plenty of rain in the Southern colonies provided colonists with seven or eight months of growing season.

By 1700, Virginia was the largest English colony. With the help of black slave labor, the Southern colonists built huge **plantations**. They became wealthy farmers who grew tobacco, wheat, rice, and **indigo**.

Name _____

Directions: Read each question carefully. Darken the circle for the correct answer.

---

1 Virginia's nickname is the Old Dominion State, but it is also known as the –

   A Five Presidents State

   B Mother of Presidents

   C New World

   D Lost Colony State

2 What was the name of the first colony in Virginia?

   F Chesapeake Bay

   G Virginia Company

   H Roanoke Island

   J Jamestown

3 The colonists were told to <u>cultivate</u> mulberry trees so they could grow silkworms. <u>Cultivate</u> means –

   A won victory over

   B chosen or selected

   C prepare the soil for growing crops

   D groups of fruit or nut trees

4 After reading about the Powhatan Confederacy, you get the idea that –

   F John Smith was the chief of the Powhatan Confederacy

   G the Powhatan Confederacy chose to build their villages near plenty of water

   H everyone in the Powhatan Confederacy spoke a different language

   J only one family lived in each Powhatan village

5 Why was the marriage between Pocahontas and colonist John Rolfe so important?

   A The marriage brought peace between the colonists and the Native Americans.

   B Pocahontas was the only Native American who spoke English.

   C After the marriage, John Smith was able to leave the colony.

   D Pocahontas was finally able to teach the colonists how to grow corn.

6 What can you learn by reading about Virginia's first black settlers?

   F They were treated the same as white settlers.

   G They did not have the same rights and freedoms as white settlers.

   H They were involved in Virginia's first government.

   J They started the first churches in Virginia.

7 Which statement about Governor Berkeley is <u>true</u>?

   A He helped the colonists fight against the Native Americans.

   B He was the king of England.

   C He would not let the colonists elect new leaders to the House of Burgesses.

   D He was a kind leader, loved by all.

READING

Answers

1 Ⓐ Ⓑ Ⓒ Ⓓ   5 Ⓐ Ⓑ Ⓒ Ⓓ
2 Ⓕ Ⓖ Ⓗ Ⓙ   6 Ⓕ Ⓖ Ⓗ Ⓙ
3 Ⓐ Ⓑ Ⓒ Ⓓ   7 Ⓐ Ⓑ Ⓒ Ⓓ
4 Ⓕ Ⓖ Ⓗ Ⓙ

Use the blank map of the thirteen original colonies to make a study guide. As you study each colony, find and label the colony on the map. Color the New England colonies blue, the Middle colonies green, and the Southern colonies red. Your study guide will help you prepare for a quiz on the thirteen original colonies.

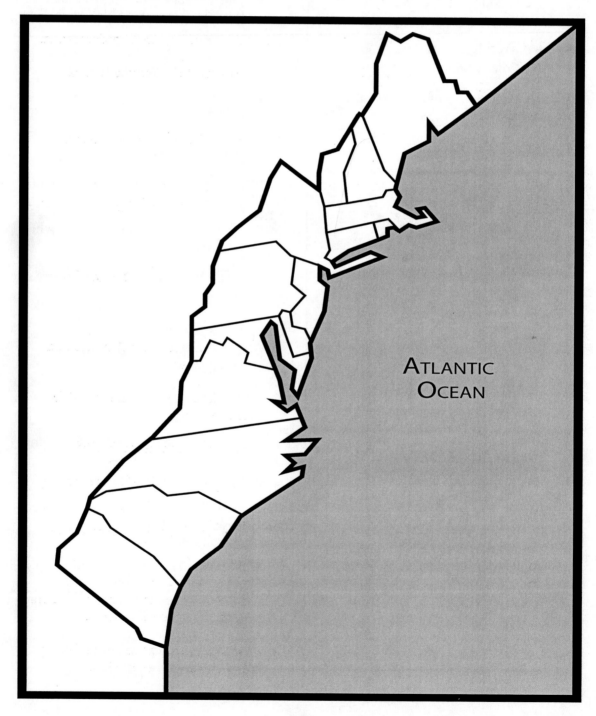

✩ ✦ ✩ ✦★ VOCABULARY QUIZ ✩ ★ ✩ ✦
THE THIRTEEN ORIGINAL COLONIES
PART I

Directions: Match the vocabulary word on the left with its definition on the right. Put the letter for the definition on the blank next to the vocabulary word it matches. Use each word and definition only once.

1. _____ Africa

2. _____ colonies

3. _____ dominion

4. _____ coast

5. _____ merchants

6. _____ New World

7. _____ cultivate

8. _____ inhabited

9. _____ confederacy

10. _____ wigwam

11. _____ fungus

12. _____ prosper

13. _____ representatives

14. _____ captives

15. _____ debt

16. _____ indentured servants

A.   an area of land that borders water.

B.   a disease that destroys plants.

C.   picked crops.

D.   made plans to harm someone.

E.   a violent attack.

F.   money that is owed to someone else.

G.   faithful.

H.   a person who is in charge of an area or group.

I.   a term once used to describe the continents of North America and South America.

J.   people chosen to speak or act for an entire group.

K.   acting out against authority.

L.   groups of people who are ruled by another country.

M.   a group of people with common goals.

N.   people who agreed to work for someone else in return for payment of travel expenses to America.

O.   prisoners who have been taken by force without permission.

17. _____ historians

18. _____ harvested

19. _____ defeated

20. _____ assault

21. _____ conflict

22. _____ loyal

23. _____ militia

24. _____ threatened

25. _____ revolted

26. _____ rebellion

27. _____ fertile

28. _____ climate

29. _____ plantations

30. _____ indigo

31. _____ appointed

32. _____ England

33. _____ governor

P. a group of men having some military training who are called upon only in emergencies.

Q. buyers and sellers whose goal is to make money.

R. the average weather conditions of an area over a period of years.

S. a plant which produces a blue dye.

T. chosen or selected.

U. lived or settled in a place.

V. to have success or wealth.

W. people who study history.

X. very large farms in the South where crops of cotton and tobacco were grown and slave labor was usually used.

Y. a territory with one ruler.

Z. fought against rules and laws felt to be unfair.

AA. a Native American home made of poles and covered with bark, mats, or animal skins.

BB. rich soil that produces a large number of crops.

CC. a struggle or disagreement.

DD. won victory over.

EE. to prepare the soil for growing crops.

FF. second largest continent in the world.

GG. a region located on the southern part of the island of Great Britain.

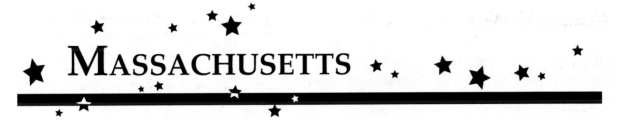

MASSACHUSETTS

Massachusetts, one of the four New England colonies, is known as the **Bay** State. It received this nickname because of an early settlement on Cape Cod Bay. Massachusetts was the home of two colonies, Plymouth and the Massachusetts Bay colony.

THE FIRST PEOPLE IN MASSACHUSETTS

Long before colonists arrived in Massachusetts, Native Americans lived there. The largest group of Native Americans in Massachusetts was a confederacy that included the Nauset (NAW•set), Nipmuc (NIP•muc), Wampanoag (wam•pu•NO•ag), and Massachuset tribes. They spoke the Algonquian (al•GONG•kee•in) language and settled in permanent villages along the rivers in Massachusetts. The confederacy also settled in the present-day city of Boston. These Native Americans hunted, fished, and grew crops of corn, beans, and squash.

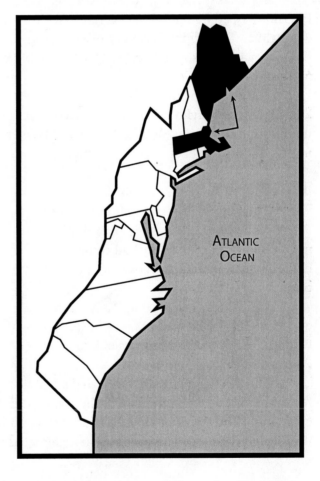

ATLANTIC OCEAN

THE PILGRIMS

The first **European** settlers in Massachusetts were the **Pilgrims**. We call them Pilgrims today, but they didn't actually receive that name until they had been in America for almost 200 years.

Before coming to America, the Pilgrims were **Puritan** farmers in England. The **Church of England** was England's **official** church. Puritans did not agree with the strict rules of the Church of England. Puritans based their lives on the Bible. They believed that human beings needed God's forgiveness to get them to heaven. They also believed that they were chosen by God to become leaders in government. The Church of England did not agree with these beliefs. Puritans wanted to find a place where they could worship freely and make important decisions.

COMING TO AMERICA

On September 6, 1620, the Pilgrims left England and sailed for America on *The Mayflower*. They were led by William Brewster. Brewster was a Puritan preacher who received money from the Virginia Company of London to start a colony in America.

The Virginia Company of London had already **founded** a successful colony in Jamestown, Virginia. In return for the money, Brewster's group promised to give the London Company part of any gold or silver found in America.

The Virginia Company of London wanted Brewster to sail toward Virginia. Stormy weather knocked *The Mayflower* off course. The Pilgrims landed in Massachusetts Bay instead of Virginia. They didn't have permission from the Virginia Company of London to settle in Massachusetts.

Before leaving their ship, the men wrote and signed the Mayflower Compact. This important document established rules and laws for the colonists to obey.

THE PLYMOUTH COLONY

The Pilgrims named their new colony Plymouth. This name was in honor of the city in England from which they had come. They elected John Carver as the governor of their colony.

The Pilgrims were completely unprepared for survival in Massachusetts. During their first winter, almost half of the Pilgrims died.

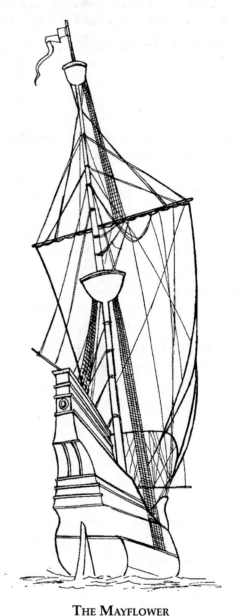

THE MAYFLOWER

The next spring, with the help of a Native American named Squanto, the Pilgrims learned to fish, hunt, and grow corn. The Pilgrims signed a peace **treaty** with the Native Americans. In the fall of 1621, the Pilgrims and the Native Americans celebrated the First Thanksgiving.

THE MASSACHUSETTS BAY COMPANY

Other settlers traveled from England to establish colonies in Massachusetts. In 1629, King Charles I of England allowed a group of wealthy businessmen to start a colony between the Charles River and the Merrimack River in Massachusetts. They called themselves the Massachusetts Bay Company.

The Massachusetts Bay Company planned to make money by setting up the first trading business in North America. The businessmen also wanted to grant religious freedom to its settlers. During the next thirteen years, more than 20,000 Puritans traveled to New England in search of religious freedom.

KING PHILIP'S WAR

As the colonies grew, there were more white settlers than Native Americans. The Native Americans feared they would be forced from their land.

In 1675, members of the Wampanoag tribe angered the English colonists. The colonists had allowed their cattle to roam freely. The cows **trampled** the corn crops of the Native Americans. The Native Americans killed the cattle. The colonists who owned the cattle became very angry. They got even by killing a Native American. These events led to King Philip's War.

King Philip, a powerful Wampanoag chief, led his people in a revolt against the colonists. The Native Americans burned many towns in Connecticut and Massachusetts. They **kidnapped** colonists. The colonists were stronger than King Philip and his troops. They captured King Philip's wife and son and sold them into slavery. In 1676, King Philip was hunted down and killed. Native Americans who survived were sold into slavery. Their land in the New England colonies was taken over by the colonists.

KING PHILIP

THE ECONOMY OF THE NEW ENGLAND COLONIES

Colonists who settled in the New England colonies found rocky soil and thick forests. The New England colonists faced long, cold winters, and short, hot summers. The growing season was only four or five months long. Most of the colonists had small farms, but the soil was poor for growing crops.

The New England colonies did offer many **harbors**. Most colonists fished, built ships, and used their location on the Atlantic Ocean to ship products to and from other colonies and England.

Name _____

Directions: Read each question carefully. Darken the circle for the correct answer.

1   **Who lived in Massachusetts before the arrival of colonists?**

   A   Native Americans

   B   Spanish explorers

   C   Colonists from Virginia

   D   French settlers

2   **Why did the Pilgrims travel to America?**

   F   They were searching for gold.

   G   There wasn't enough room in England for them anymore.

   H   They were searching for religious freedom.

   J   They got lost trying to find Asia and ended up in America by accident.

3   **After reading about the Pilgrims' journey to America, you get the idea that –**

   A   they didn't have any leaders in their group

   B   they were actually on their way to Virginia, not Massachusetts

   C   they paid for their own trip to America

   D   there were no rules or laws established for their colony

4   **Which phrase about the Plymouth Colony tells you that the Pilgrims were unprepared for life in America?**

   F   ...named their colony Plymouth...

   G   ...elected John Carver as governor...

   H   ...during their first year, almost half the Pilgrims died...

   J   ...in 1621, the Pilgrims and the Native Americans celebrated the First Thanksgiving...

5   **The Massachusetts Bay Company planned to make money in America by –**

   A   selling land to the Native Americans

   B   granting religious freedom to its settlers

   C   growing tobacco to ship back to England

   D   setting up the first trade business in North America

6   **All of the following statements about King Philip's War are true <u>except</u> –**

   F   the war started because a colonist shot a cow belonging to a Native American

   G   the Native Americans were led by King Philip

   H   King Philip died during the war

   J   the colonists won the war and took the land once owned by the Native Americans

7   **What type of climate was found in the New England colonies?**

   A   Short winters and long hot summers.

   B   Cool summers and warm winters.

   C   Long cold winters and short hot summers.

   D   Warm dry summers and short cool winters.

READING

Answers

1 Ⓐ Ⓑ Ⓒ Ⓓ   5 Ⓐ Ⓑ Ⓒ Ⓓ

2 Ⓕ Ⓖ Ⓗ Ⓙ   6 Ⓕ Ⓖ Ⓗ Ⓙ

3 Ⓐ Ⓑ Ⓒ Ⓓ   7 Ⓐ Ⓑ Ⓒ Ⓓ

4 Ⓕ Ⓖ Ⓗ Ⓙ

Grid Math is a fun way to learn an important skill. Grids are used to find places on maps, to track weather patterns, and in space exploration.

For Example: If you want to draw a box where D meets C (D,C), you would go <u>over</u> to D and <u>up</u> to C, and draw the box in that space. On a map or an atlas, (D,C) may be the place where you would find the name of a city.

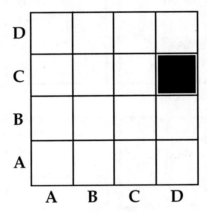

Directions: In this activity you will use a grid system to put together a puzzle that should remind you of an event in Massachusetts's history. You will need the 48 puzzle pieces (some of the puzzle pieces are below and the rest of them are on the next page), and the blank grid.

1. Cut out the puzzle pieces **one at a time** (cut around the thick black line of the square). Glue **that** piece in its proper place on the empty grid before cutting out the next piece. Make sure that you do not turn the puzzle piece upside down or turn it on its side before gluing it; the way it looks before you cut it out is the way it should be glued onto the grid.

2. Follow the example above: If the puzzle piece is labeled **(D,A)**, glue that piece in the space where D meets A on the grid by going <u>over</u> to D and <u>up</u> to A.

3. When you are finished, color in your picture with your coloring pencils.

4. **(D,A)** has been done for you as an example.

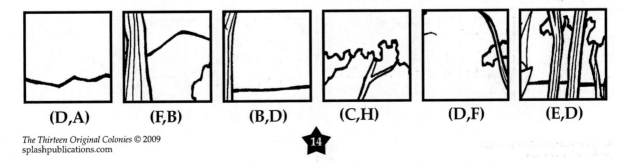

(D,A)   (F,B)   (B,D)   (C,H)   (D,F)   (E,D)

(E,G)   (B,H)   (C,B)   (D,E)   (C,F)   (A,G)

(C,E)   (D,B)   (E,H)   (A,D)   (C,G)   (E,C)

(F,G)   (B,E)   (F,E)   (A,B)   (C,D)   (B,G)

(E,F)   (A,H)   (F,F)   (D,D)   (E,B)   (C,A)

(F,H)   (B,C)   (F,A)   (A,F)   (B,B)   (D,C)

(E,E)   (F,C)   (A,A)   (B,F)   (E,A)   (D,G)

(C,C)   (A,E)   (F,D)   (B,A)   (A,C)   (D,H)

	A	B	C	D	E	F
H						
G						
F						
E						
D						
C						
B						
A						

NEW HAMPSHIRE

New Hampshire, the **Granite** State, was one of the four New England colonies. New Hampshire's nickname comes from the state's many granite **formations** and deposits.

NEW HAMPSHIRE'S FIRST PEOPLE

More than 12,000 Native Americans who spoke the Algonquian (al•GONG•kee•in) language inhabited New Hampshire before the arrival of European explorers. About half of these people belonged to the Pennacook tribe.

The Pennacook lived in the Merrimack River Valley of New Hampshire. They were farmers who lived in permanent villages. The Pennacook also hunted during the year. During the summer, some members of the tribe traveled to the **seacoast** to fish and gather shellfish.

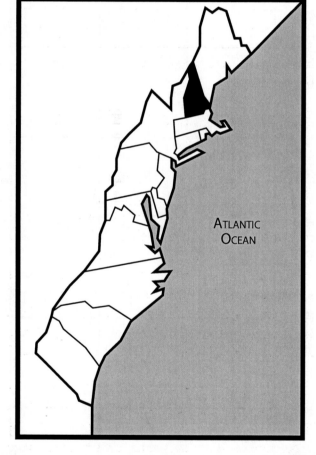

ATLANTIC OCEAN

NEW HAMPSHIRE'S EXPLORERS

In 1603, the first recorded visit to New Hampshire was made. English sea captain Martin Pring explored the **shoreline** and a small area of New Hampshire's **interior**.

Pring was hired by some wealthy merchants in England to travel to America. They hoped he would find a shortcut to **Asia**. The wealthy businessmen also wanted Pring to bring back American plants and roots that could cure colds and other illnesses. Pring did not find the plants or the easy route to Asia. He did find an area that was full of forests and fur-bearing animals. Pring was not interested in establishing any permanent settlements in New Hampshire.

In 1605, **French** explorer Samuel de Champlain (sham•PLANE) visited New Hampshire. Like Pring, Champlain was also searching for a water route to Asia. Champlain made maps of the New England coastline for France.

JOHN SMITH

English explorer John Smith had already helped establish England's first American colony in Jamestown, Virginia. In 1609, Smith was badly injured in a gunpowder explosion. He left Virginia and returned to England for medical care.

In 1614, John Smith got the chance to return to America. He was hired to lead an English whale-hunting, fishing, and fur-trading **expedition** to what is now the northeastern United States.

On this trip to America, Smith explored the coast of New Hampshire. He made notes about the land, people, plants, and animals. John Smith named the area he visited New England. He drew the first good maps of the New England area.

John Smith returned to England and wrote books about his adventures in America. He **encouraged** other English colonists to travel to America. He warned them that it would take a lot of hard work and **determination** to settle in America.

JOHN SMITH

SETTLEMENTS IN NEW HAMPSHIRE

In 1623, New Hampshire's first permanent settlements were founded. A few settlers arrived from **Scotland**. They established farms, fishing villages, and a trading post in the present-day town of Rye located on the Atlantic Coast. Settlers from London arrived a few years later and built a settlement north of Rye in Dover. By 1638, other settlements had been established in the present-day cities of Portsmouth, Exeter, and Hampton.

The Native Americans were friendly to the Europeans and even taught them many survival skills. With the help of the Native Americans, the European settlers learned how to grow corn, tap maple trees for syrup, and make canoes. The Native Americans also taught the settlers where to find the best hunting places. In return, the Europeans gave the Native Americans metal tools, blankets, and weapons. The weapons were valuable for hunting and protection from enemy tribes.

From the early 1640s until 1679, the New Hampshire towns were under the leadership of the Massachusetts Bay Colony. This group had already established a colony in Massachusetts. The Massachusetts Bay Colony developed a system of government and protection for its settlers. No new settlements were established in New Hampshire during this time. Only one exploration was made, which led to the discovery of the White Mountains.

A ROYAL COLONY

In 1680, New Hampshire became a royal colony. The king of England selected a president and a **council** for the colony. Conflicts arose between New Hampshire and Massachusetts over land **boundaries**. The leaders in the Massachusetts Bay Colony gave land in New Hampshire to its settlers. The settlers in New Hampshire claimed that this land belonged to them. The New Hampshire settlers felt that the Massachusetts Bay Colony had no right to give the land away.

In 1686, King James II took away the colonists' right to make their own laws and rules. He angered the New England colonists when he joined New Hampshire, Massachusetts, Rhode Island, Connecticut, New Jersey, and New York into a single **province**. He named the province the Dominion of New England. King James II appointed Sir Edmund Andros governor of the province.

Sir Edmund Andros was a mean governor. He taxed the colonists of the province and used the money to become wealthy. Anyone who refused to pay the taxes was sent to jail. In the spring of 1689, the colonists captured Governor Andros and threw him in jail. Andros was sent back to England. The New England colonists took charge of the province and once again started making their own laws and rules.

NATIVE AMERICAN CONFLICTS IN NEW HAMPSHIRE

Other New England colonies were constantly at war with the Native Americans. The settlers in New Hampshire maintained peaceful relationships with the Native peoples. This changed as the population of New Hampshire grew. New Hampshire's settlers took control of Native American hunting and fishing territories. The new settlers brought **livestock** with them. The livestock grazed on the crops in the Native Americans' fields. This angered the Native Americans.

The English settlers wanted control of the land in New Hampshire. The French wanted control of New Hampshire's hunting territories. The Native Americans in New Hampshire were already angry with the English settlers. Many of the tribes sided with the French. Together they fought to drive the English colonists from New Hampshire.

THE KING WILLIAM'S WAR

One of the most **destructive** battles of this period was the King William's War. Beginning in 1689, Native Americans attacked white settlements, burned houses, killed hundreds of settlers, and took many of the settlers captive. The women and children were marched into Canada where they were used by the French as slaves. The constant threat of Native American attacks kept the New Hampshire settlers from **expanding** into new areas. Food **production** dropped. Nearly every family in New Hampshire suffered a loss.

NEW HAMPSHIRE FIGHTS BACK

England could not afford to send the large numbers of soldiers required to fight the French and their Native American **allies**. As a result, New Hampshire and the other colonies had to provide their own soldiers to fight for the land. Several forts were built in New Hampshire to provide protection for the colony.

New Hampshire's settlers murdered thousands of Native Americans and burned their villages and crops. Even Native Americans who weren't involved in the fighting lost their lives and homes. A reward was offered for the **scalps** of Native American men, women, and children.

HANNAH DUSTIN

Hannah Dustin lived with her husband and eight children in the New Hampshire town of Haverhill. In the spring of 1697, Native Americans **raided** Haverhill. They killed about 30 people and took several prisoners.

Hannah, her newborn baby, and the baby's nurse were taken as prisoners during the raid. Shortly after leaving Haverhill, the Native Americans murdered Hannah's baby.

The Native Americans and their captives traveled more than 100 miles through New Hampshire. They planned to take their prisoners to Canada and sell them as slaves to the French. The group stopped to rest along the Merrimack River.

Hannah and two other captives grabbed the hatchets of the sleeping Native Americans. They killed and scalped ten of the Native Americans. Hannah and the other surviving prisoners took a canoe and paddled down the Merrimack River to safety.

HANNAH DUSTIN

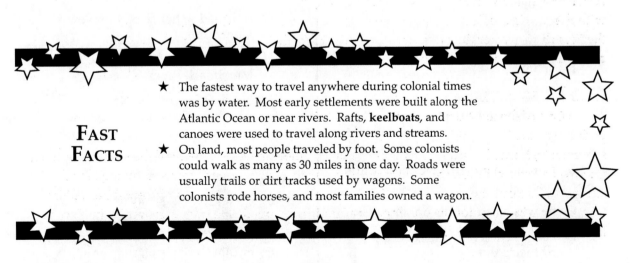

FAST FACTS

★ The fastest way to travel anywhere during colonial times was by water. Most early settlements were built along the Atlantic Ocean or near rivers. Rafts, **keelboats**, and canoes were used to travel along rivers and streams.

★ On land, most people traveled by foot. Some colonists could walk as many as 30 miles in one day. Roads were usually trails or dirt tracks used by wagons. Some colonists rode horses, and most families owned a wagon.

Name _____

Directions: Read each question carefully. Darken the circle for the correct answer.

---

1   **New Hampshire is known as the Granite State. Granite is a type of –**

   A   journey

   B   mill

   C   rock

   D   battle

2   **When Martin Pring explored America, he found –**

   F   gold and silver

   G   a shortcut to Asia

   H   plants and roots to cure illnesses

   J   forests and fur-bearing animals

3   **What can you learn from reading about John Smith?**

   A   He wanted others to travel to America.

   B   He was afraid of water.

   C   He was killed in an explosion.

   D   Nobody would hire him to explore America, so he paid for his own trip.

4   **Where did New Hampshire's first colonists come from?**

   F   France

   G   Scotland

   H   England

   J   Spain

5   **After reading about Sir Edmund Andros, you get the idea that –**

   A   he was a very poor man

   B   he tried to do what was best for the colonists

   C   he was hated for his unfair rules

   D   he was chosen by the colonists to be their leader

6   **Which statement about the King William's War is false?**

   F   England sent soldiers and supplies to help the colonists fight the war.

   G   the Native Americans killed hundreds of settlers during the war.

   H   The colonists fought back by killing Native Americans and burning their villages.

   J   Many of New Hampshire's colonists were taken to Canada and sold into slavery.

7   **In order to save her life, Hannah Dustin –**

   A   ran away from her family

   B   swam across the Merrimack River

   C   used a hatchet to scalp the Native Americans who kidnapped her

   D   hid in a closet so the Native Americans wouldn't find her

8   **Based on what you have read, if Hannah Dustin hadn't been able to escape, she probably would have –**

   F   been sold into slavery

   G   returned to her family in New Hampshire

   H   continued to live along the Merrimack River

   J   been set free by the Native Americans who kidnapped her

---

READING

Answers

1   Ⓐ Ⓑ Ⓒ Ⓓ   5   Ⓐ Ⓑ Ⓒ Ⓓ
2   Ⓕ Ⓖ Ⓗ Ⓙ   6   Ⓕ Ⓖ Ⓗ Ⓙ
3   Ⓐ Ⓑ Ⓒ Ⓓ   7   Ⓐ Ⓑ Ⓒ Ⓓ
4   Ⓕ Ⓖ Ⓗ Ⓙ   8   Ⓕ Ⓖ Ⓗ Ⓙ

☆ ✦ ☆ ✦✦ VOCABULARY QUIZ ☆ ✦ ☆ ✦✦

THE THIRTEEN ORIGINAL COLONIES
PART II

Directions: Match the vocabulary word on the left with its definition on the right. Put the letter for the definition on the blank next to the vocabulary word it matches. Use each word and definition only once.

1. _____ European

2. _____ Pilgrims

3. _____ raided

4. _____ scalps

5. _____ allies

6. _____ official

7. _____ founded

8. _____ expanding

9. _____ destructive

10. _____ livestock

11. _____ province

12. _____ treaty

13. _____ boundaries

14. _____ council

15. _____ Scotland

16. _____ Church of England

A. the tops of human heads that are usually covered with hair.

B. a journey for the purpose of exploring.

C. animals raised on a farm to eat or sell for profit.

D. a hard rock formed millions of years ago that contains crystals.

E. gave support, courage, or hope to someone.

F. land that borders the sea.

G. a person who comes from the continent of Europe.

H. the inside of something.

I. dividing lines.

J. sheltered areas of water deep enough to provide ships a place to anchor.

K. proper or correct.

L. the edge of a body of water.

M. the world's largest continent with more than half of the Earth's population.

N. walked heavily on something and crushed or destroyed it.

O. causing damage.

17. _____ trampled

18. _____ determination

19. _____ encouraged

20. _____ kidnapped

21. _____ bay

22. _____ expedition

23. _____ French

24. _____ harbors

25. _____ keelboats

26. _____ granite

27. _____ formations

28. _____ seacoast

29. _____ shoreline

30. _____ Asia

31. _____ interior

32. _____ Puritan

33. _____ production

P.   a person from England who traveled to America in the 1600s and 1700s in search of religious freedom.

Q.   the English colonists who founded the first permanent settlement in the New England colony of Plymouth in 1620.

R.   a formal agreement.

S.   groups of people who come together to help one another in times of trouble.

T.   a group of people chosen to make laws or give advice.

U.   started or established.

V.   a part of a country having a government of its own.

W.   arrangements of something.

X.   the official church in England.

Y.   the act of making something.

Z.   one of the four countries that make up Great Britain and Northern Ireland; famous for bagpipes and plaid skirts known as kilts.

AA. growing larger.

BB. a person from France, a country in western Europe.

CC. making a decision and sticking to it, no matter how difficult.

DD. shallow covered river boats that are usually rowed or towed and used for carrying supplies.

EE. took someone without permission.

FF. suddenly attacked.

GG. a body of water surrounded by land that opens to the sea.

New York

New York, one of the four Middle colonies, is known as the **Empire** State. President George Washington had great dreams for New York. He saw New York as the "seat of empire." Today, New York is the home of the Empire State Building.

New York's First People

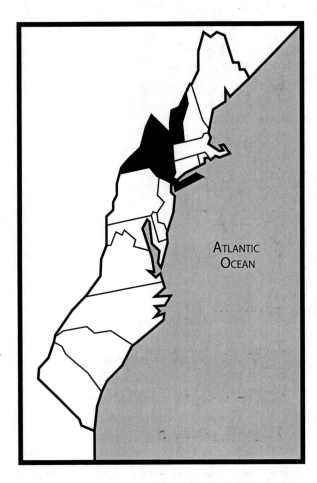

Native Americans lived in New York long before the first English colonists arrived. Tribes that spoke the Iroquois (EAR•uh•kwoy) and Algonquian (al•GONG•kee•in) languages were the two major groups of Native Americans who made their homes in New York.

The Algonquian-speaking peoples included the Mahican (muh•HEE•kun), Delaware, and Pequot (PEE•kwat) tribes. They were farmers and hunters who lived in wigwams throughout the Hudson River Valley, Manhattan, and Long Island.

Tribes that spoke the Iroquois language controlled the rest of the New York area. They were known as the League of Five Nations. The League included the Mohawk, Seneca, Oneida (oh•NIE•duh), Cayuga (kay•YOU•guh), and Onondaga (on•un•DAW•guh) tribes.

The Iroquois were hunters and farmers. They grew corn, squash, beans, pumpkins, and tobacco. They also raised **orchards** of apples and peaches. The Iroquois called themselves "people of the **longhouse**." They built longhouses made of bark and logs. Each longhouse was up to 200 feet in length and home to several Iroquois families at the same time. Some of the pottery and tools made by the Iroquois and Algonquian-speaking tribes are **preserved** in New York's museums today.

ATLANTIC OCEAN

HENRY HUDSON

Henry Hudson was an English explorer and a sea captain. He made four different **voyages** searching for the Northwest Passage. The Northwest Passage was a water route that explorers hoped connected **North America** to Asia.

Getting to Asia was very important to European explorers like Henry Hudson. In Asia, they could buy jewels, silk, and spices that were not available in Europe. The only way to get these items was to buy them from Italian traders. The Italian traders purchased the items in Asia and sold them at very high prices to Europeans. If explorers found a water route to Asia, they could buy the things they wanted without paying Italian traders anything.

Like other explorers before him, Henry Hudson was more interested in finding the Northwest Passage than he was in settling the New World.

During Hudson's first two voyages, he sailed northeast along the coast of **Greenland**. He was only 700 miles from the **North Pole**. No other explorer had ever sailed so far north. Unfortunately, huge pieces of ice blocked his way. Both times, Hudson and his small crew were forced to return to England.

HENRY HUDSON

SAILING TO NORTH AMERICA

In 1609, Henry Hudson made his first of two voyages to North America. Sailing for the **Dutch**, Hudson once again tried to find the Northwest Passage. He sailed as far south as the present-day state of North Carolina. He also turned his ship north and explored the Chesapeake and Delaware bays. Hudson traveled up what became known as the Hudson River to the present-day city of Albany in New York.

THE HUDSON BAY

In 1610, a group of English merchants supplied Henry Hudson with a ship for another voyage to the New World. Again, Hudson searched for the Northwest Passage. It was during this expedition that Hudson discovered bodies of water that were later named Hudson **Strait** and Hudson Bay.

Hudson mistakenly thought he had found the Pacific Ocean. Ice formed on the water. Hudson's crew was forced to spend the winter in the southern end of the Hudson Bay. The crew suffered from cold, hunger, and disease. They were so angry with Hudson that they threw him, his son, and a few members of his crew off the ship. Hudson and his group were never seen again.

DUTCH CONTROL OF NEW YORK

Henry Hudson's voyages to North America allowed the Dutch to claim the entire Hudson River Valley. This land stretched through the present-day states of New York, New Jersey, Connecticut, and Delaware. The Dutch named this territory New Netherland. In 1614, the Dutch built Fort Nassau (NAH•saw). The Dutch used Fort Nassau as a place to trade with the Native Americans. In 1617, Fort Nassau was destroyed by a flood.

THE FUR TRADE

The colonists from England weren't the only settlers in the New World. While the English colonists established permanent settlements along the Atlantic Ocean, French colonists settled in the **Great Lakes** area. Both groups were interested in gaining more land for their countries. They also wanted to take control of the beaver hunting and trading territories.

Beaver furs were worth a lot of money to the colonists. The smooth, waterproof beaver furs were shipped back to France and England where they were sold for a very high **profit**. Everyone in these countries wanted a beautiful hat or coat made of beaver fur. The French and English colonists would do anything to protect this business.

Native Americans in the Great Lakes area trapped beaver and traded with the French colonists. Native Americans who lived along the Atlantic Ocean trapped and traded with the English and Dutch colonists.

The trade relationship between the Dutch settlers and the Native Americans caused great conflicts in New Netherland. The Native Americans hunted the beaver. They traded the beaver furs with the settlers. The settlers gave the Native Americans European goods, metal tools, and weapons. Of course, all of the Native Americans in New Netherland wanted to trade with the Dutch settlers. There simply wasn't enough beaver in the area for everyone to hunt and trade. Wars often resulted. The Iroquois tribes usually won because they were the strongest and most organized groups of Native Americans in New Netherland.

NEW AMSTERDAM

In 1624, another group of Dutch colonists built the first permanent settlement in present-day New York. The Dutch named this settlement New Amsterdam. Peter Minuit was chosen as New Amsterdam's governor. In 1626, Governor Minuit purchased present-day Manhattan from the Native Americans for just twenty four dollars. Other Dutch settlements were soon started in the area. Problems with leadership and conflicts with the Native Americans did not stop new settlers from coming to the area to farm. Soon churches and schools were built in the Dutch colonies.

ENGLISH CONTROL OF NEW YORK

In 1664, England took control of New Netherland. England's King Charles II gave the colony to his brother, the Duke of York. Afraid of going to war with England, the Dutch signed a treaty and gave up New Amsterdam as well. In honor of the Duke, the entire area was renamed New York. New York offered freedom of religion to all **Christians**. The right to vote was granted to all white land owners. New York City soon became a busy **seaport** that attracted people from many different countries.

THE ECONOMY OF THE MIDDLE COLONIES

The Middle colonies offered plenty of natural **resources** that included rich farmland and thick forests. The climate of the Middle colonies was not as harsh as the climate found in the New England colonies. Farmers enjoyed plenty of rain in the summer and a long growing season.

The Hudson and Delaware rivers provided plenty of fresh fish. The colonists learned how to turn water from these rushing rivers into energy that they could use. Water power was used to cut lumber in their **sawmills**. They also put water power to use in their **gristmills** for making flour.

FAST FACTS

★ Everyone in a colonial family worked. This included children and adults. Children were expected to get out of bed and get dressed before the sun came up in the morning. Each child from the youngest to the oldest had chores to do. Making their beds, feeding the farm animals, planting crops, and cutting firewood were some of the jobs done by colonial children.

★ At meal time, colonial children did not sit at the main table with their parents. Sometimes they stood behind an adult who handed them food. In other homes, children sat at a separate table with the servants or at the end of the table. Colonial children were expected to eat silently and quickly without asking any questions.

Name _____

Directions: Read each question carefully. Darken the circle for the correct answer.

1 After reading about New York's first people, you learn that –

A the English colonists were already in New York when the Native Americans arrived

B tribes were separated by the languages that they spoke

C the Delaware people built longhouses where many families lived at the same time

D New York's first people did very little farming

2 Why was finding a shortcut to Asia so important to explorers like Henry Hudson?

F Explorers wanted to claim land in Asia and build settlements.

G Asia offered things that weren't available in Europe.

H There were fur-bearing animals in Asia.

J They were searching for religious freedom that Asia offered.

3 What can you learn from reading about Henry Hudson?

A He sailed farther north than any other explorer before him.

B He found the Northwest Passage.

C His crew thought he was a great leader who deserved honor and respect.

D After spending the winter in the Hudson Bay, he returned to England and wrote a book about his adventures.

4 If Henry Hudson was English, why did the Dutch claim the entire Hudson River Valley?

F Hudson sold the Hudson River Valley to the Dutch.

G The Dutch purchased the Hudson River Valley from the Native Americans.

H The Dutch wanted the Hudson River Valley, so they just took it.

J Since Henry Hudson was paid by the Dutch to explore, the land he discovered belonged to the Dutch.

5 After reading about the fur trade, you can conclude that –

A there was enough beaver for everyone to participate in the profitable fur trade

B without the Native Americans, the fur trade probably wouldn't have been very successful

C it was very difficult to trap beaver

D beaver furs weren't worth very much to the Native Americans

6 Based on what you have read, if you had been a child living in a colony, you <u>probably</u> would have –

F played with your friends all day

G told stories at the dinner table

H slept until the sun woke you

J eaten at a different table from your parents

Answers

READING

1 Ⓐ Ⓑ Ⓒ Ⓓ   4 Ⓕ Ⓖ Ⓗ Ⓙ
2 Ⓕ Ⓖ Ⓗ Ⓙ   5 Ⓐ Ⓑ Ⓒ Ⓓ
3 Ⓐ Ⓑ Ⓒ Ⓓ   6 Ⓕ Ⓖ Ⓗ Ⓙ

HOW-TO-DRAW
A BEAVER

During colonial days, beaver furs were very profitable for the colonists. The skins were shipped to France and England where they were made into expensive fur hats. There were many conflicts between the colonists and the Native Americans over beaver hunting territories. In this activity, you will follow written directions to draw a beaver.

Directions: Very lightly sketch out the first step. Then, also very lightly add step 2. Continue in this way until all four steps are completed. In each drawing, the new step is shown darker than the step before it so that the lines can be clearly seen. You should keep your drawing very light.

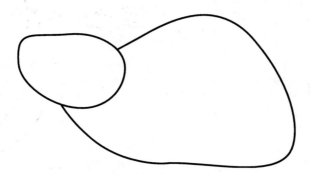

1. Draw these shapes to form the head and body.

2. Add lines to form the legs, the feet, and the tail.

3. Add lines to form the nose, the eye, the ear, the mouth, the teeth, and the feet.

4. Erase guidelines, smooth out other lines, and add detail.

Color

Use your black coloring pencil to trace the outline of the teeth, nose, whiskers, eye, and tail of your beaver. Color the nose, eye, and tail black. Then use your brown coloring pencil to trace the outline of the beaver. Lightly color your beaver brown.

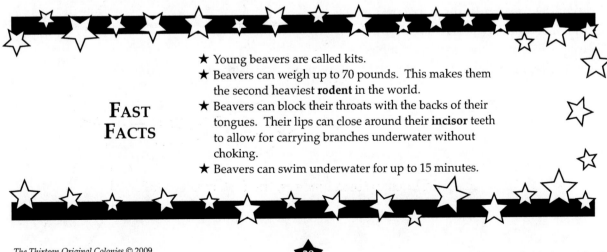

Fast Facts

★ Young beavers are called kits.
★ Beavers can weigh up to 70 pounds. This makes them the second heaviest **rodent** in the world.
★ Beavers can block their throats with the backs of their tongues. Their lips can close around their **incisor** teeth to allow for carrying branches underwater without choking.
★ Beavers can swim underwater for up to 15 minutes.

MARYLAND

Maryland, one of the five Southern colonies, is known as the Free State. This nickname fits Maryland because colonists who settled in Maryland were looking for, and found, religious freedom.

Another nickname, suggested by General George Washington, was the Old Line State. Washington suggested this name because he **admired** the way Maryland's troops fought during the **Revolutionary War**.

MARYLAND'S FIRST PEOPLE

Native Americans who spoke the Algonquian (al•GONG•kee•in) language inhabited Maryland long before Europeans arrived.

In 1526, Spanish explorers first visited the area now known as Maryland. They sailed into the Chesapeake Bay and named the area Santa Maria.

In 1608, John Smith of Virginia was the first English visitor to the territory. More than 20 years later, in 1631, William Claiborne and other **Protestants** from Virginia set up a fur-trading post on Kent Island, just off the eastern shore of the Chesapeake Bay. These settlers established a trading relationship with several Native American groups who lived in the area.

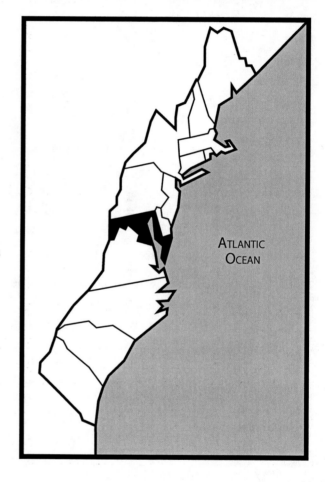

ATLANTIC OCEAN

GEORGE CALVERT

In 1632, King Charles I of England granted a large area of land near the Chesapeake Bay to George Calvert. The colony was to be named Maryland in honor of the king's wife, Henrietta Maria. George Calvert wanted to find a place where Roman **Catholics** could worship freely. Catholics were not allowed to practice their religion in England. They were often arrested for doing so.

William Claiborne and the other Protestant settlers living beside the Chesapeake Bay were not very happy that George Calvert was going to start a colony of Catholics in Maryland.

In 1632, George Calvert died. He was not able to make his dream of religious freedom for Catholics a reality. His son, Cecil Calvert, was granted the **charter** instead.

ST. MARY'S

On March 24, 1634, Cecil Calvert's brother Leonard and 200 colonists arrived on Saint Clement Island at the mouth of the Potomac River. Cecil wanted to join them on the voyage, but he had to stay in England. Instead, he sent Leonard and made him governor of the colony. Governor Calvert and his colonists purchased the Native American village of Yaocomico (ya•co•ME•co). They changed the name of the village to St. Mary's.

GEORGE CALVERT

About 25 of the colonists who traveled with Calvert paid their own way for the trip. These wealthy families were given land. They also paid the way for others to join them in Maryland. These people became indentured servants who had to work on the wealthy land owners' plantations for seven years before earning their freedom.

CONFLICTS IN MARYLAND

Disease and hunger caused many deaths in the colony's first few years. Almost every child lost at least one parent during this difficult time. Leonard Calvert returned to England in 1644. During the two years that he was gone, the colony went through more **turmoil**. There was constant fighting between the Protestants and the Catholics.

St. Mary's was used for 60 years as the capital and center of Calvert's colony. Governor Calvert welcomed Roman Catholics and all non-Catholic Christians to his colony. In 1649, Maryland's government passed the Act Concerning Religion. This was the first **statute** in the colonies to allow Christians the freedom to practice their religion and own land.

William Claiborne and his group of Protestants built a settlement at Providence. The **quarreling** between the Protestants and the Catholics continued. Finally, in 1692, England took complete control of Maryland. England established the Church of England as the official religion. The colonists were taxed to pay for the church.

Name _____

Directions: Read each question carefully. Darken the circle for the correct answer.

---

1 **Why does the nickname Free State fit Maryland so well?**

  A Everything in Maryland was free.

  B Black slaves were taken to Maryland when they were set free.

  C Colonists found religious freedom in Maryland.

  D The Native Americans gave free land to Maryland's first settlers.

2 **What can you learn by studying the map of the thirteen original colonies?**

  F Maryland is the northernmost of the thirteen colonies.

  G Each of the thirteen colonies borders the Pacific Ocean.

  H Maryland is the southernmost of the thirteen colonies.

  J Each of the thirteen colonies borders the Atlantic Ocean.

3 **George Washington <u>admired</u> the way Maryland's troops fought during the Revolutionary War. <u>Admired</u> means –**

  A thought highly of

  B chosen or selected

  C groups of people who come together to help one another in times of trouble

  D faithful

4 **Why did George Calvert want to establish a colony in Maryland?**

  F He wanted to make money trading beaver furs with the Native Americans.

  G He had always wanted to live beside the Atlantic Ocean.

  H He wanted to find a place where Catholics could worship freely.

  J He hoped to find silver and gold in Maryland.

5 **After reading about St. Mary's, you get the idea that –**

  A it wasn't a very good place for farming

  B many of the settlers had a lot of money

  C the Native Americans were forced to give up their land to the white settlers

  D Cecil Calvert was the first person to step off the ship when they arrived at St. Mary's

6 **There was a lot of <u>turmoil</u> between the Protestants and Catholics living in Maryland. <u>Turmoil</u> means –**

  F friendship

  G confusion

  H trading

  J kindness

Answers   **READING**

1 Ⓐ Ⓑ Ⓒ Ⓓ   4 Ⓕ Ⓖ Ⓗ Ⓙ

2 Ⓕ Ⓖ Ⓗ Ⓙ   5 Ⓐ Ⓑ Ⓒ Ⓓ

3 Ⓐ Ⓑ Ⓒ Ⓓ   6 Ⓕ Ⓖ Ⓗ Ⓙ

Name _____

the source

Think about the resources we use to learn about history. Reading books, seeing movies, looking at photographs, studying maps, searching the Internet, digging for bones, and holding pieces of pottery are some of the ways that we learn about the past.

There are two types of sources to help us learn about what happened in the past. Primary sources are recorded by people who were there at the time. If you have ever read a diary or an **autobiography**, then you were reading something that was written by the person who was actually recording the events and experiences as they were happening. Diaries and autobiographies are primary sources. Letters, interviews, photographs, original maps, bones, and pieces of pottery are other examples of primary sources because they give us "first-hand" knowledge of an event that took place in history.

Secondary sources are recorded by people after an event took place. Many books have been written about important historical events and people. A book written in 2005 about the life of Maryland settler Leonard Calvert is a secondary source because the author wasn't actually there to interview the famous settler and can't give any "first-hand" knowledge. Movies, **biographies**, newspaper stories, and encyclopedias are other examples of secondary sources because they give us "second-hand" knowledge of events that took place in history.

You have just finished studying about the first English colonies. The colonists who traveled to the New World were some of the first people to explore, settle, and begin America's history.

In this activity, you will decide whether a source of information is a primary source or a secondary source. On the lines provided, put a "P" next to the primary sources and an "S" next to the secondary sources.

1. _____ A story about Roanoke Island's "Lost Colony" written by one of your classmates.

2. _____ A model of a Powhatan wigwam displayed in a Virginia museum.

3. _____ The diary one of the first Pilgrims wrote describing his voyage to the New World.

4. _____ A piece of wood preserved from the actual *Mayflower*.

5. _____ John Smith's autobiography.

6. _____ An encyclopedia article written about the Revolutionary War.

7. _____ The map that Henry Hudson drew of the Hudson River.

✦ ✦ ✦ ✦✦ VOCABULARY QUIZ ✦ ✦ ✦ ✦✦
THE THIRTEEN ORIGINAL COLONIES
PART III

Directions: Match the vocabulary word on the left with its definition on the right. Put the letter for the definition on the blank next to the vocabulary word it matches. Use each word and definition only once.

1. _____ empire

2. _____ orchards

3. _____ longhouse

4. _____ quarreling

5. _____ statute

6. _____ turmoil

7. _____ biographies

8. _____ charter

9. _____ Catholics

10. _____ preserved

11. _____ voyages

12. _____ North America

13. _____ admired

14. _____ rodent

15. _____ Greenland

16. _____ Revolutionary War

A. a contract which gives one group power over another.

B. groups of fruit or nut trees.

C. a narrow strip of sea between two pieces of land.

D. protected from injury or ruin so more could be learned.

E. battle for independence between the English colonists in America and Great Britain.

F. members of a Christian church other than the Roman Catholic Church.

G. a rule or law.

H. mills for grinding grain into flour.

I. businesses with big machines that saw wood into planks and boards.

J. thought highly of.

K. long dwelling where many Native American families live at the same time.

L. the story of your life written by you.

M. small mammal with large front teeth used for gnawing or nibbling.

N. members of a Christian church who trace their history back to the twelve apostles.

17. _____ North Pole

18. _____ gristmills

19. _____ Dutch

20. _____ strait

21. _____ profit

22. _____ Christians

23. _____ seaport

24. _____ Great Lakes

25. _____ Protestants

26. _____ incisor

27. _____ autobiography

28. _____ resources

29. _____ sawmills

O. journeys that are usually made by water.

P. people who are from the Netherlands, a country of northwest Europe on the North Sea.

Q. arguing and fighting.

R. money made after all expenses have been paid.

S. a sheltered area where ships can load and unload supplies.

T. one of seven continents in the world. Bounded by Alaska on the northwest, Greenland on the northeast, Florida on the southeast, and Mexico on the southwest.

U. constant confusion and disorder.

V. the northernmost point on the Earth.

W. the world's largest island. Located northeast of North America.

X. one of four front cutting teeth in the upper or lower jaw.

Y. five large lakes located in North America at the border between Canada and the United States. The names of the lakes are Superior, Michigan, Huron, Erie, and Ontario.

Z. things found in nature that are valuable to humans.

AA. stories of a person's life written by someone else.

BB. people who belong to a religion based on the life and teachings of Jesus Christ.

CC. a group of territories or peoples under one ruler.

The Thirteen Original Colonies © 2009
splashpublications.com

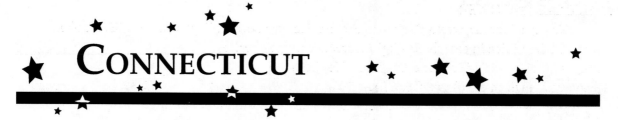

CONNECTICUT

Connecticut, the southernmost of the four New England colonies, is known as the **Constitution** State. In 1639, colonists in Connecticut **adopted** the nation's first written constitution. This is why Connecticut is nicknamed the Constitution State.

CONNECTICUT'S FIRST PEOPLE

Native Americans inhabited Connecticut long before any other people visited the area. They spoke the Algonquian (al•GONG•kee•in) language. Algonquian tribes in Connecticut included the Pequot (PEE•kwat), the Mohegan (mo•HEE•gun), the Niantic (nye•AN•tick), the Mahican (muh•HEE•kun), and the Siwanog (SEE•wah•nog).

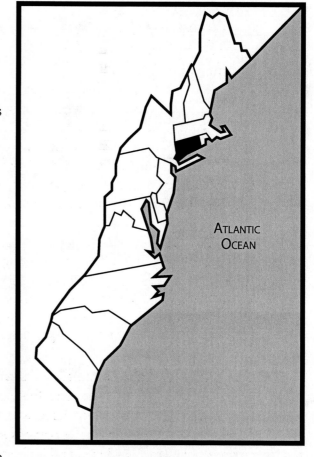

The Pequot was the most powerful and feared Algonquian tribe. In the early 1600s, there were about 20,000 Native Americans living in Connecticut. They survived by hunting deer and fishing. They also grew crops of corn, beans, and tobacco. Native Americans in Connecticut lived in wigwams. These were dome-shaped houses made of poles, tree bark, and grass.

DUTCH FUR TRADERS

Historians believe that the first white explorer in Connecticut was Adriaen Block. He was a Dutchman from the Netherlands. In 1614, Block explored the Connecticut River.

The Dutch were not really interested in establishing permanent settlements in Connecticut. They were interested in trading with the Native Americans.

The Dutch gave the Native Americans European tools and metal weapons. In return, the Native Americans gave the Dutch beaver furs. The furs were taken back to Europe where they were sold for a very high price. Hats and other pieces of clothing were made out of the beaver furs. To protect their profitable fur trade from other European groups, the Dutch built a fort in the present-day city of Hartford.

THOMAS HOOKER

Thomas Hooker was a Puritan preacher. He was born in England. In 1633, Hooker traveled to America in search of religious freedom. In America, Thomas Hooker settled in Massachusetts. He did not always agree with the colony's leaders.

Hooker believed that each church should be **independent**. He also felt that the people of each church had the right to choose the colony's leaders and decide what powers those leaders should have.

The leaders in Massachusetts disagreed with Hooker. They felt that only the leaders of the Puritan church should choose leaders for the colony.

In 1636, Thomas Hooker and a group of 100 colonists left Massachusetts. They moved to Connecticut and started a new colony. Hooker made positive changes in his colony. All church members, not just church leaders, chose the colony's leaders.

Together with other English colonists who moved from Massachusetts, Hooker's group built the towns of Hartford, Wethersfield, and Windsor. These towns were called the "Three River Towns" because they were located on the Connecticut River.

Most of the Native Americans were friendly to the English colonists living in Connecticut. Instead of just taking the land from the Native Americans, Hooker and his followers purchased the land in Connecticut.

THOMAS HOOKER

THE PEQUOT WAR

During the 1630s, two things happened that destroyed the peace between Connecticut's Native Americans and the colonists. Control of the fur trade was the first struggle. The Pequot controlled the fur trade throughout New England. They decided which tribes could trade with the white settlers and the price that would be paid for the furs. The Pequot refused to allow the colonists to control the **wampum** and the fur trade in New England. This made the colonists very angry.

In 1634 and 1636, colonists killed two members of the Pequot tribe. The Pequot captured the murderers and refused to let them go. Fighting broke out after a colonist **accused** a Pequot of murder. The colonists declared war on the Pequot.

In the spring of 1637, the colonists attacked the main Pequot village. With the help of the Narragansett (nar•ra•GAN•set) and Mohegan tribes, they burned the Pequot village. Hundreds of Native American men, women, and children were killed as they tried to escape. The Pequot who survived were captured and taken to **Bermuda** where they were sold into slavery.

THE FIRST CONSTITUTION

In 1639, the people of the Three River Towns **united** as one colony. They wrote their own set of laws known as the Fundamental Orders of Connecticut. Some believe that this was the first written constitution in the New World. The Fundamental Orders established an independent government that made laws for **elections**, courts, powers of officials, and taxes. It gave all white men who owned land the power to vote.

CONTROL OF CONNECTICUT

In 1662, Charles II was the king of England. King Charles II established Connecticut as an independent colony. He also gave the Connecticut Colony a charter. The charter gave the colonists more control over their government. King Charles II permitted the Connecticut Colony to control all of the land in present-day Connecticut.

In 1685, King Charles II died. His brother, James II, became the king of England. King James II wanted more control over the colonies in America. He took away Connecticut's power to rule itself. In 1686, King James II united Connecticut with other nearby colonies. The new colony was called the Dominion of New England.

THE CHARTER OAK

King James II appointed a royal governor for the Dominion of New England. His name was Sir Edmund Andros. In 1687, Andros demanded that Connecticut give up its charter. The leaders of Connecticut refused. They hid Connecticut's charter in a hollow oak tree. This tree became known as the Charter Oak. It stood for Connecticut's love of freedom.

By 1689, King James II had been **overthrown**. The colonists sent Sir Edmund Andros back to England. Connecticut once again became a separate colony.

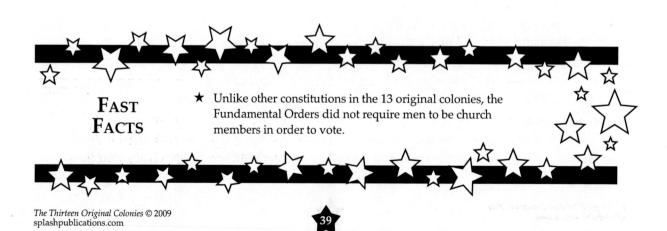

FAST FACTS

★ Unlike other constitutions in the 13 original colonies, the Fundamental Orders did not require men to be church members in order to vote.

Name _____

Directions: Read each question carefully. Darken the circle for the correct answer.

1 Of all the Native Americans living in Connecticut, which tribe was the most feared?

A The Mohegan

B The Niantic

C The Iroquois

D The Pequot

2 What did the Dutch want to do in Connecticut?

F Search for gold.

G Build settlements.

H Find religious freedom.

J Trade with the Native Americans.

3 Before settling in Connecticut, Thomas Hooker lived in –

A France

B Virginia

C Massachusetts

D Spain

4 Which phrase about Thomas Hooker best describes why he moved to Connecticut?

F ...did not always agree with the colony's leaders...

G ...was a Puritan preacher...

H ...Hooker and a group of 100 colonists left Massachusetts...

J ...built the towns of Hartford, Wethersfield, and Windsor...

5 The Native Americans who survived the Pequot War were –

A given back their land

B sold into slavery

C thrown in prison

D sent to England

6 According to the Fundamental Orders, who was permitted to vote?

F Anyone who lived in Connecticut.

G Women and men who paid taxes.

H Everyone except Native Americans and blacks.

J White men who owned property.

7 What can you learn by reading about King James II?

A He thought exactly like his brother, King Charles II.

B He and his brother felt very differently about the power that the colonists should have.

C He was only interested in the colonists' happiness.

D The colonists liked King James II better than his brother Charles.

READING

Answers

1 Ⓐ Ⓑ Ⓒ Ⓓ   5 Ⓐ Ⓑ Ⓒ Ⓓ

2 Ⓕ Ⓖ Ⓗ Ⓙ   6 Ⓕ Ⓖ Ⓗ Ⓙ

3 Ⓐ Ⓑ Ⓒ Ⓓ   7 Ⓐ Ⓑ Ⓒ Ⓓ

4 Ⓕ Ⓖ Ⓗ Ⓙ

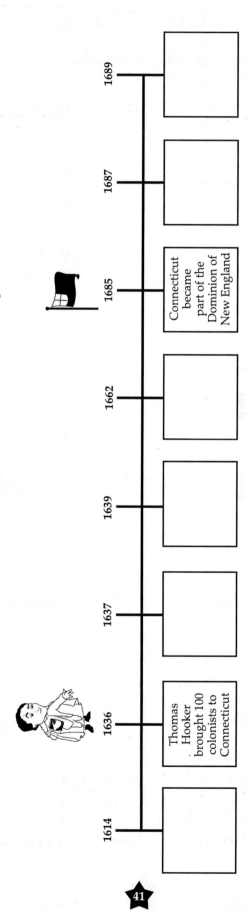

A time line is a tool used to list dates and events in the order that they happened. The time line below lists important dates in Connecticut's colonial history. Notice that many of the events are missing.

1614 — 1636 Thomas Hooker brought 100 colonists to Connecticut — 1637 — 1639 — 1662 — 1685 Connecticut became part of the Dominion of New England — 1687 — 1689

PART I

Directions: In the first part of this activity, you will use your information about Connecticut to fill in the missing events on the time line. Then, choose the picture that you think best represents each event. Color and cut out each picture before gluing it into its proper spot on the time line. Since you were not present for any of these events, this time line would be a **secondary source**.

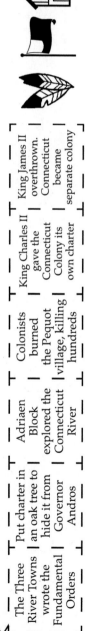

| The Three River Towns wrote the Fundamental Orders | Put charter in an oak tree to hide it from Governor Andros | Adriaen Block explored the Connecticut River | Colonists burned the Pequot village, killing hundreds | King Charles II gave the Connecticut Colony its own charter | King James II overthrown. Connecticut became separate colony |

PART II

Directions: In the second part of this activity, you will create a time line of your life by listing the dates and events in order as they happened. Since you are supplying the information about your own life, your time line would be considered a **primary source**.

1. Use the boxes drawn below to make a time line of your life. Put the dates in the top boxes and the events in the bottom boxes.

2. The first date of your time line should be your birth. The last date should be the most recent event in your life.

3. Try to list only the important events of your life. If you list one important event for each year of your life, you will easily use all of the boxes. You may even add more boxes on the back if you need more room.

4. On a separate piece of paper, choose one of the events from the time line and draw a picture of it.

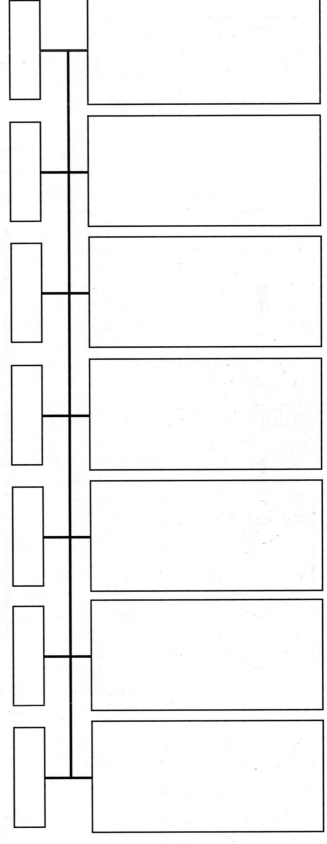

RHODE ISLAND

Rhode Island, one of the four New England colonies, is known as Little Rhody or the Ocean State. Rhode Island was the smallest of the thirteen original colonies. In fact, with a land area of only 1,212 square miles, Rhode Island is the smallest state in the Union.

The nickname Little Rhody was chosen because of Rhode Island's small size. However, the Ocean State is Rhode Island's official nickname. Rhode Island's location on the Atlantic Ocean makes it easy to understand why it is known as the Ocean State.

RHODE ISLAND'S FIRST PEOPLE

Five Native American tribes that spoke the Algonquian (al•GONG•kee•in) language inhabited Rhode Island before Europeans visited the area. The largest and most powerful group was the Narragansett (nar•ra•GAN•set) tribe. About 5,000 members of this tribe lived in eight different villages throughout Rhode Island.

Other Native Americans in Rhode Island included the Niantic (nye•AN•tick), Wampanoag (wam•puh•NO•ag), Pequot (PEE•kwat), and the Nipmuc (NIP•muc). These Native Americans farmed, hunted deer, fished, and gathered shellfish from the Atlantic Ocean.

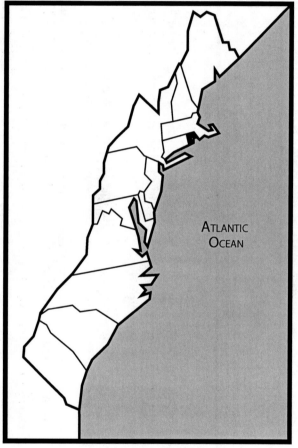

ATLANTIC
OCEAN

ROGER WILLIAMS

Roger Williams was an important part of Rhode Island's history. He was not the first European to visit Rhode Island, but he did establish the first permanent settlement in the area.

Roger Williams was a Puritan preacher who lived in the Massachusetts Bay Colony.

ROGER WILLIAMS

Like others, he traveled to America in search of religious freedom. He did not agree with the leadership of the Massachusetts Bay Colony and he refused to be quiet about it. Williams did not think the government should tell people how to practice their religion. He firmly believed that Puritans should not be able to start a colony in North America until they purchased the land from the Native Americans.

In 1635, Roger Williams was ordered to leave Massachusetts. At first he refused. Then he found out that a group of men were coming to force his family to return to England. He left his wife and two daughters in Massachusetts and went to Rhode Island.

Roger Williams was welcomed by the leader of the Wampanoag tribe. The Native Americans gave him food and shelter. After learning their ways and their language, he bought land from them.

PROVIDENCE

In 1636, Williams and a few followers began building a town on the land purchased from the Wampanoag tribe. He quickly learned that the land was already claimed by the Plymouth Colony in Massachusetts. Williams did not want to cause trouble between the Plymouth Colony and the Massachusetts Bay Colony. Instead, he purchased nearby land from the Narragansett tribe. It was here that he started Rhode Island's first permanent settlement.

Roger Williams named the settlement Providence. Providence means God's guidance. He chose this name because he felt God had provided a place for him and others to worship freely. Providence was the first colony to welcome people of all religions and **nationalities**. As a result, Rhode Island was the site of the first Jewish **synagogue** (SIN•uh•gog), the first Baptist church, and one of the first **Quaker** meeting houses.

ANNE HUTCHINSON

Roger Williams was not the only colonist who had difficulties in Massachusetts. While Williams was busy building his colony in Rhode Island, Anne Hutchinson was being arrested for speaking out in Massachusetts.

Anne Hutchinson was born in England. She arrived in Boston, Massachusetts at the age of 43. Like Roger Williams, Anne Hutchinson and her family traveled to America in search of religious freedom. She quickly found that the church run by the Massachusetts Bay Colony offered less religious freedom than the churches in England.

In Massachusetts, Anne quickly became a town leader. She nursed the sick and helped deliver babies. Hutchinson had 15 children of her own. Anne Hutchinson also led church meetings in her home. It was during these meetings that she caused the most trouble for the Puritan church.

It was believed that leading church meetings was a man's job. Women were supposed to keep quiet during church services and look after their children. She taught other women that they could pray to God without the help of a preacher. This went completely against the laws of the Puritan church.

In 1638, Anne Hutchinson was forced to leave the Massachusetts Bay Colony. With her family and a small group of followers, she traveled to Rhode Island. Roger Williams helped the group purchase land from the Native Americans in Rhode Island's present-day city of Portsmouth.

ANNE HUTCHINSON

Anne continued her message in Portsmouth. She held church meetings in her home and taught colonists that God's love was for everyone. After her husband died, Anne moved to New York. In 1643, she was murdered by Native Americans.

FAST FACTS

★ Anne Hutchinson learned to speak out at a very young age. Her father was a church leader in England. He was thrown in jail for speaking out against the leadership of that church.

★ The Puritan church established by the leaders of the Massachusetts Bay Colony believed that men were smarter than women. Reading, writing, and studying were things that men did. Women cooked, cleaned, and took care of the children.

Name _____

RHODE ISLAND

Directions: Read each question carefully. Darken the circle for the correct answer.

---

1 **Why was the nickname Little Rhody chosen for Rhode Island?**

  A The roadrunner is Rhode Island's state bird.

  B The rhododendron is Rhode Island's state flower.

  C Rhode Island is the smallest state in the Union.

  D There are many roads in Rhode Island.

2 **Roger Williams is an important part of Rhode Island's history because–**

  F he was the first European to visit Rhode Island

  G he discovered gold in Rhode Island

  H he wrote a book about Rhode Island

  J he established Rhode Island's first permanent settlement

3 **Which phrase about Roger Williams best shows that he felt strongly about his beliefs?**

  A ...refused to be quiet about it...

  B ...traveled in search of religious freedom...

  C ...gave him food and shelter...

  D ...began building a town...

4 **Rhode Island was the site of the first synagogue. Which religion uses a synagogue?**

  F Catholic

  G Protestant

  H Christian

  J Jewish

5 **Why was Anne Hutchinson arrested in Massachusetts?**

  A She robbed a bank.

  B She killed someone.

  C She spoke out about her beliefs.

  D She was delivering babies.

6 **After reading about Anne Hutchinson's religious beliefs, you get the idea that –**

  F she believed that women could be just as active in church leadership as men

  G she believed only men should lead church services

  H she agreed with the laws of the Puritan church

  J she believed that women should keep quiet and take care of their children

7 **What did the leaders of the Puritan church believe about men and women?**

  A They believed that women were smarter than men.

  B They believed that men and women were equal.

  C They believed that men were smarter than women.

  D They believed that women should study hard to be as smart as men.

READING

Answers

1 Ⓐ Ⓑ Ⓒ Ⓓ   5 Ⓐ Ⓑ Ⓒ Ⓓ

2 Ⓕ Ⓖ Ⓗ Ⓙ   6 Ⓕ Ⓖ Ⓗ Ⓙ

3 Ⓐ Ⓑ Ⓒ Ⓓ   7 Ⓐ Ⓑ Ⓒ Ⓓ

4 Ⓕ Ⓖ Ⓗ Ⓙ

Roger Williams and Anne Hutchinson were two of Rhode Island's most famous colonists.

In this activity, you will collect facts about Roger Williams or Anne Hutchinson to make a game known as "Find the Fib."

Directions:

1. Choose either Roger Williams or Anne Hutchinson to make the game "Find the Fib."
2. Use your scissors to cut apart the Roger Williams or Anne Hutchinson "Find the Fib" cards given to you by your teacher. You will need 20 cards.
3. Neatly color the pictures of Roger Williams or Anne Hutchinson on each card.
4. Use information about Roger Williams and Anne Hutchinson, encyclopedias, books in the library, the Internet, and other **primary** and **secondary** sources to find 15 true facts about the colonist you have chosen.
5. Write each fact on a separate card. Try to fit the whole fact on one side of the card.
6. Make up 5 false facts, or "fibs" about your chosen colonist. Make the fib as believable as possible so that it can't be easily seen as a fib.
7. Write each fib on a separate card, just like you did with the true facts. Again, try to fit the whole fib on one side of the card.
8. Mix and shuffle all of the cards together, so the true facts and fibs are mixed together.
9. Number the cards 1-20.
10. Make an answer key for yourself so you will know which cards are the true facts and which cards are the fibs.
11. Give your cards to 2 or 3 other people in the class to see if they can find the true facts and the fibs.

SAMPLE CARD

FRONT | BACK

1

In 1636, Roger Williams established Rhode Island's first permanent settlement.

ANNE HUTCHINSON FIND THE FIB CARDS

DELAWARE

Delaware, one of the four Middle colonies, is known as the First State. The nickname fits so well because Delaware was the first of the thirteen original colonies to become a state.

DELAWARE'S FIRST PEOPLE

Native Americans were the first people to inhabit Delaware. In 1624, Dutch explorers from the Netherlands arrived in Delaware. They found a group of Native Americans living along the Delaware River.

The Dutch explorers named these people Delaware Indians. The Native Americans called themselves Lenni-Lenape (len•AH•pay). Lenni-Lenape means "original people," or "real people."

The Delaware lived in wigwams and hunted and fished. They also grew crops of corn, beans, and squash. The Delaware Indians were frightened by the Dutch explorers.

DUTCH COLONISTS

In 1631, the Dutch built the first settlement in Delaware. They planned to make money hunting whales and making whale oil.

Unfortunately, the Dutch colony only lasted one year. It was completely destroyed after a disagreement with the nearby Native Americans of the Lenni-Lenape tribe.

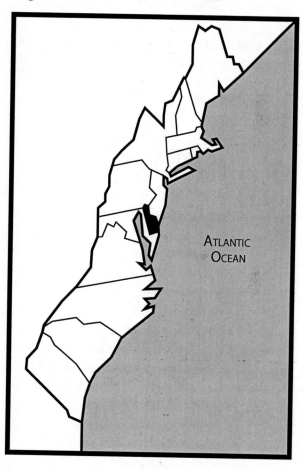

ATLANTIC OCEAN

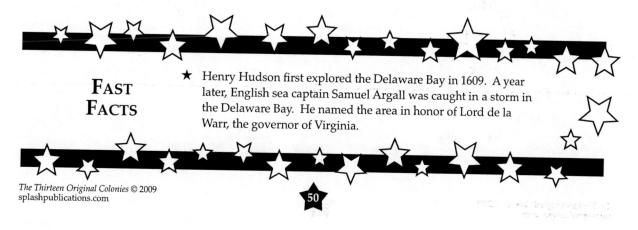

FAST FACTS

★ Henry Hudson first explored the Delaware Bay in 1609. A year later, English sea captain Samuel Argall was caught in a storm in the Delaware Bay. He named the area in honor of Lord de la Warr, the governor of Virginia.

New Sweden

In 1638, a group of Swedish settlers purchased land in Delaware from the Dutch. A Swedish colony was established at Fort Christina. The area surrounding the colony was named New Sweden. The Swedish **pioneers** in Delaware were the first group of people in America to build log cabins.

In 1655, the Dutch returned to Delaware and captured Fort Christina. The Swedes were forced to give up New Sweden to the Dutch. The Dutch did not remain in control for very long. In 1664, England **seized** all of the Dutch territory in America.

The Dutch settlers who already lived in Delaware were permitted to keep their land and property as long as they **pledged** their loyalty to the king of England. Delaware changed ownership a few more times before England took final control of the land in 1674.

Swedish Log Cabin

The Pennsylvania Province

In 1682, the Duke of York gave William Penn a piece of territory in present-day Delaware. Penn already had a colony in nearby Pennsylvania, but Pennsylvania had no seaport. William Penn asked the Duke of York for more land along the coast of the Atlantic Ocean. The Duke of York gave Penn the land on the west bank of the Delaware River.

Penn named his entire piece of land the Pennsylvania Province. William Penn wanted everyone in his colony to be free and happy. He paid the Delaware people for their land. In 1682, William Penn signed a treaty of friendship with the Native Americans.

Some of the colonists in the southern part of the Pennsylvania Province were not pleased with Penn's leadership. He was a Quaker. Not everyone agreed with his religious beliefs. The colonists were worried that the area was growing too quickly. They were also angry that Penn was not able to stop **pirate** raids on their settlements along the shore. In 1704, these settlers broke away and formed the separate colony of Delaware.

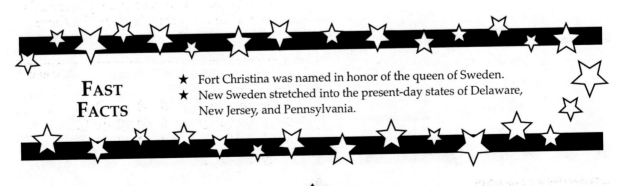

Fast Facts

★ Fort Christina was named in honor of the queen of Sweden.
★ New Sweden stretched into the present-day states of Delaware, New Jersey, and Pennsylvania.

Name _____

Directions: Read each question carefully. Darken the circle for the correct answer.

1 The nickname First State fits Delaware so well because –

A it was the first of the thirteen original colonies to become a state

B it was the first state to have Native Americans living in it

C it was the first colony visited by explorers

D it was the first colony to allow women to vote

2 The Native Americans in Delaware called themselves Lenni-Lenape. Lenni-Lenape means –

F "by the river"

G "real people"

H "wigwam dwellers"

J "brave warriors"

3 The Dutch settlers in Delaware planned to make money by –

A trading with the Lenni-Lenape

B selling land to future colonists

C growing tobacco and indigo

D hunting whales and making whale oil

4 The Swedish settlers in Delaware were the first people to build –

F longhouses

G wigwams

H log cabins

J teepees

5 In 1664, England <u>seized</u> all of the Dutch territory in America. <u>Seized</u> means –

A borrowed

B took

C bought

D sold

6 Why did William Penn want land in Delaware when he already had a successful colony in nearby Pennsylvania?

F Penn wanted all of the land he could get.

G Pennsylvania did not have a seaport and Penn wanted land along the coast of the Atlantic Ocean.

H Penn was not happy in Pennsylvania and he wanted to move to Delaware.

J Penn wanted to build a bigger house and he didn't have enough room in Pennsylvania.

7 The colonists in the southern part of the Pennsylvania Province were not pleased with Penn's leadership for all of the following reasons <u>except</u> –

A he was a Quaker

B he was allowing the area to grow too quickly

C he was mean to the Native Americans

D he wasn't able to stop the pirate raids on their settlements along the shore

READING

Answers

1 Ⓐ Ⓑ Ⓒ Ⓓ   5 Ⓐ Ⓑ Ⓒ Ⓓ

2 Ⓕ Ⓖ Ⓗ Ⓙ   6 Ⓕ Ⓖ Ⓗ Ⓙ

3 Ⓐ Ⓑ Ⓒ Ⓓ   7 Ⓐ Ⓑ Ⓒ Ⓓ

4 Ⓕ Ⓖ Ⓗ Ⓙ

FOLLOWING DIRECTIONS
MAKING A LOG CABIN

In this activity you will make a miniature log cabin just like the kind built by Delaware's Swedish colonists.

Materials: Scissors, glue, coloring pencils, and log cabin pattern.

1. Color the log cabin.

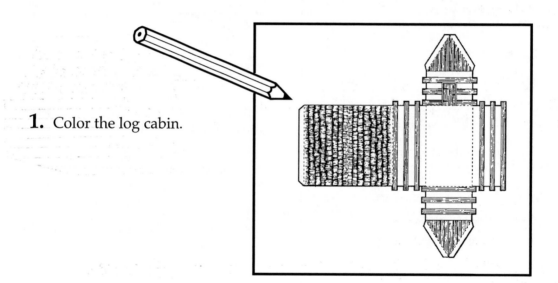

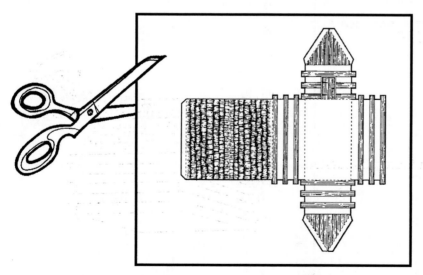

2. Cut out the log cabin along the bold black lines. It is <u>very important</u> that you do not cut off the bold black lines.

3. Make folds along all of the dotted black lines.

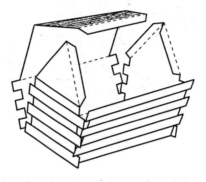

4. Pull interlocking tabs to connect each corner.

5. Glue all of the tabs marked **A** to the inside of the roof .

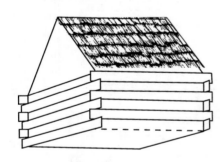

6. Tuck tab **B** into the opposite side.

7. Glue tab **B** to the side where it is tucked.

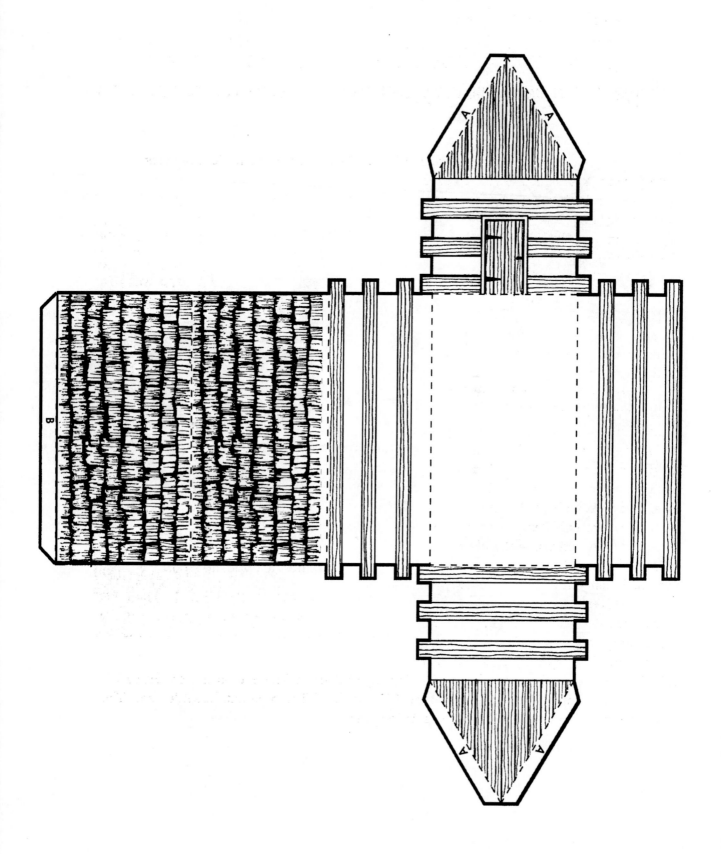

PENNSYLVANIA

Pennsylvania, the Quaker State or Keystone State, was one of the four Middle colonies. Pennsylvania was nicknamed the Quaker State because William Penn, a Quaker, founded a colony in Pennsylvania.

Pennsylvania is known as the Keystone state because it is located in the center of the thirteen original colonies.

PENNSYLVANIA'S FIRST PEOPLE

Long before white settlers arrived in Pennsylvania, it was home to about 15,000 Native Americans.

Most of Pennsylvania's Native Americans belonged to tribes that spoke the Iroquois (EAR•uh•kwoy) and Algonquian (al•GONG•kee•in) languages. These tribes included the Susquehannock (sus•kwuh•HAN•ock), Erie, Delaware, and the Shawnee.

The forests of Pennsylvania gave these Native Americans material for building houses. The rivers and fertile soil provided them with plenty of food.

In 1614, the Dutch explored the lands along the Delaware River. In 1643, the territory was named New Sweden by a party of Swedish explorers. The Swedish

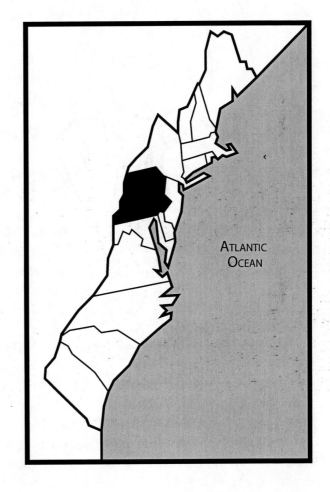

ATLANTIC OCEAN

colonies were established near the present-day city of Chester. These colonies were the first permanent settlements in Pennsylvania. In 1655, Dutch soldiers captured the settlement. The Dutch controlled Pennsylvania for the next nine years.

QUAKERS IN PENNSYLVANIA

In 1682, William Penn founded the first English colony in Pennsylvania. Penn belonged to a religious group known as the Quakers, or the Society of Friends. The Quakers believed that all people were equal. They also took very seriously the Bible's **Commandment** that states, "Thou shalt not kill." Because of this Commandment, the Quakers would not fight in war.

The Quakers also refused to pay taxes that were used to pay for war. These beliefs did not make the Quakers very popular with the government in England. Many Quakers, including William Penn, were thrown in jail for their beliefs.

WILLIAM PENN

WILLIAM PENN'S HOLY EXPERIMENT

William Penn promised that if he ever got out of prison he would start a colony where Quakers could live in peace. In 1681, he was granted 28 million acres of land in North America by his friend, King Charles of England. This was one of the largest land grants ever given to an individual.

A year later, Penn arrived in Pennsylvania with 100 Quakers to start what he called a "Holy Experiment." They settled on a piece of land along the Delaware River. Penn named the place Philadelphia, which means "brotherly love" in Greek.

THE GREAT LAW OF PENNSYLVANIA

William Penn kept true to his promise that all men were equal. He established the "Great Law of Pennsylvania." This law granted men who believed in God and owned property the right to vote.

Penn treated the Native Americans with kindness. He even paid them for their land. He signed a treaty of friendship with the Native Americans. William Penn made sure that the laws of his colony were fair. Penn's motto was "Mercy, Justice, Truth, Peace, Love, Plenty."

William Penn's "Holy Experiment" worked. Pennsylvania became one of the leading colonies in America. By 1700, there were more than 4,000 settlers in Pennsylvania. They owned some of the most successful farms, businesses, and trading companies in the thirteen original colonies.

Name _____

Directions: Read each question carefully. Darken the circle for the correct answer.

---

1 **Why is Pennsylvania known as the Quaker State?**

  A Quakers have never been permitted to live in Pennsylvania.

  B A colony in Pennsylvania was founded by Quaker William Penn.

  C There have been more earthquakes in Pennsylvania than in any other state.

  D Quakers are the only people living in Pennsylvania today.

2 **What did the first Native Americans use for building houses in Pennsylvania?**

  F Rocks and sticks.

  G Mud from the Delaware River.

  H Wood from the forest's trees.

  J Animal skins.

3 **After reading about Pennsylvania's first people, you get the idea that –**

  A it was the only place in America without Native Americans living in it

  B Pennsylvania's first people had difficulty finding food

  C the Dutch established Pennsylvania's first colony

  D the Swedish established Pennsylvania's first colony

4 **William Penn belonged to a religious group known as the Quakers. The Quakers were also known as –**

  F William Penn's Religion

  G the Group Against War

  H the Society of Friends

  J Roman Catholics

5 **The Quakers lived by the Ten <u>Commandments</u>. <u>Commandments</u> are –**

  A rules

  B debts

  C colonies

  D charters

6 **What can you learn from reading about William Penn's "Holy Experiment?"**

  F Penn traveled to Pennsylvania by himself.

  G The "Holy Experiment" took place in Massachusetts.

  H Penn named the settlement Mississippi, which means "love and kindness" in Spanish.

  J Penn received the land for his experiment from a very powerful friend.

7 **All of the following were part of William Penn's motto for his colony <u>except</u> –**

  A follow

  B truth

  C plenty

  D mercy

READING

Answers

1 Ⓐ Ⓑ Ⓒ Ⓓ   5 Ⓐ Ⓑ Ⓒ Ⓓ

2 Ⓕ Ⓖ Ⓗ Ⓙ   6 Ⓕ Ⓖ Ⓗ Ⓙ

3 Ⓐ Ⓑ Ⓒ Ⓓ   7 Ⓐ Ⓑ Ⓒ Ⓓ

4 Ⓕ Ⓖ Ⓗ Ⓙ

Geography is the study of the Earth. It includes the Earth's land, water, weather, animal life, and plant life. **Geographers** are people who study geography. You can think of yourself as a geographer because you will be learning about places on the Earth.

Location is important to the study of geography. It is almost impossible to figure out your location or find your way around if you do not know the four main, or **cardinal directions.** North, south, east, and west are the **cardinal directions**. On a map these directions are labeled N, S, E, and W.

COMPASS ROSE

Between the four main directions are the **intermediate directions.** Northeast, or NE, is the direction between north and east. Southeast, or SE, is the direction between south and east. Southwest, or SW, is the direction between south and west. Northwest, or NW, is the direction between north and west.

A **reference point** is also important for finding your location. A **reference point** is simply a starting point. It's difficult, for example, to travel southwest if you don't have a starting point.

Example: The Carnegie Museum of Natural History is one of four Carnegie museums in this city. Favorite **exhibits** include Native American pottery, insects, and a hands-on dinosaur fossil dig. The Carnegie Hall Museum of Natural History is <u>southwest</u> of <u>Clarion</u>.

This example gives you some very important information. It tells you that your **reference point**, or starting point, will be the city of Clarion. Locate Clarion on your Pennsylvania map. Put your finger on Clarion and slide it <u>southwest</u>. You should see a picture of the Carnegie Museum of Natural History already placed there for you.

Sometimes directions contain more than one **reference point**. Look at the example below:

Example: Hersheypark is a chocolate-coated candy kingdom and world class amusement park. Each year, more than two million visitors find thrilling rides, a North American wildlife park, and streets with names like cocoa and chocolate. Hersheypark is <u>southeast</u> of <u>Altoona</u> and <u>southwest</u> of Reading.

This example contains two **reference points** and two sets of directions. They have been underlined for you. Look at your Pennsylvania map. Put your finger on the city of Altoona and slide it <u>southeast</u>. Since there are many points of interest located southeast, a second **reference point** has been added to help you find your location.

The second **reference point** is Reading. Place your finger on Reading and slide it <u>southwest</u>. By using both of these **reference points**, you should be able to easily locate Hersheypark.

Directions: In this activity you will use reference points, cardinal directions, and intermediate directions to plot important points of interest on a Pennsylvania map. Many of these points of interest preserve history. This helps historians learn more about the people who lived before us.

1.   Use your coloring pencils to color the symbols on the bottom of the last page. Carefully cut out the symbols.

2.   Label the cardinal and intermediate directions on the compass rose drawn for you on the Pennsylvania map.

3.   Use the written directions and your compass rose to correctly locate these points of interest on your Pennsylvania map.

4.   To get you started, the reference points and directions have been underlined for you in the first five descriptions. You may want to underline the reference points and directions in the rest of the activity.

5.   Glue the symbols in their proper places on your map. (Glue the symbols right over the dots.)

6.   When you have finished, use your coloring pencils to add more color to your Pennsylvania map.

1. The Sky's the Limit Ballooning offers visitors a different view of Pennsylvania. Drift through the skies, float over **meadows**, and brush the treetops in a hot air balloon. The Sky's the Limit Ballooning is <u>northwest</u> of <u>Hersheypark</u> and <u>southeast</u> of <u>Clarion</u>.

2. The Allegheny National Forest covers more than 500,000 acres and offers enough outdoor recreation for everyone to enjoy. There are more than 1,000 miles of hiking, biking, horseback riding, and cross-country skiing trails available in the forest. The Allegheny National Forest is <u>north</u> of <u>Clarion</u>.

3. The Pennsylvania Heritage Festival is an **annual** event that offers visitors a look into the history and **culture** of this region. Each year, the festival includes a large display of antique wagons, cars, and tractors. The festival also preserves the memory of the underground railroad that helped black slaves escape to freedom in the North and the **Civil War**. The Pennsylvania Heritage Festival is <u>north</u> of <u>Williamsport</u>.

4. Bushkill Falls is known as the "Niagara of Pennsylvania." Excellent hiking trails and bridges lead visitors to the eight waterfalls hidden deep within the forested areas of the Pocono Mountains. Bushkill Falls is <u>northeast</u> of Reading and <u>southeast</u> of <u>Williamsport</u>.

5. Fireman's Hall Museum is a fun place to learn about the history of fire fighting and fire safety tips. The museum is located within a 1902 fire house filled with equipment and hands-on exhibits. Fireman's Hall Museum is <u>south</u> of <u>Bushkill Falls</u>.

6. The Erie Zoo features animal and plant collections from all over the world. Visitors can travel as far as Africa and Asia without ever leaving Pennsylvania. Gorillas, warthogs, pythons, zebras, and toucans are just a few of the animals seen at the Erie Zoo. The Erie Zoo is northwest of the Allegheny National Forest.

7. Steamtown National Historic Site preserves the history of steam-powered trains. Visitors will feel the heat from the firebox, hear the bells and whistles from the trains, and smell the hot steam and oil as the engines roar back to life. Steamtown National Historic Site is southeast of the Pennsylvania Heritage Festival.

8. In the winter of 1777, during the Revolutionary War, General George Washington took his American soldiers to Valley Forge. Bitter cold, poor clothing, and little food made for a horrible experience. The only good thing to come out of the terrible winter was that a German officer volunteered to train the American soldiers at Valley Forge. In the spring of 1778, the American troops left Valley Forge well trained and ready to fight. Valley Forge is southeast of Hersheypark.

9. Oil Region National Heritage Area preserves the history of the first successful oil well, drilled in 1859, by Edwin L. Drake. Known today as "the valley that changed the world," visitors board the Oil Creek & Titus Railroad to get a closer look at oil **artifacts** and life in Oil City. Oil Region National Heritage Area is southwest of the Allegheny National Forest.

10. Mt. Davis is the highest mountain in Pennsylvania. The peak is 3,213 feet above sea level and can be reached by driving or following one of several hiking trails. The area is home to bobcats, black bears, and many different bird **species**. Mt. Davis is southeast of the Carnegie Museum of Natural History.

The Sky's the Limit Ballooning

Allegheny National Forest

Pennyslvania Heritage Festival

Bushkill Falls

Fireman's Hall Museum

Erie Zoo

Steamtown National Historic Site

Valley Forge

Oil Region National Heritage Area

Mt. Davis

Name _____

PENNSYLVANIA

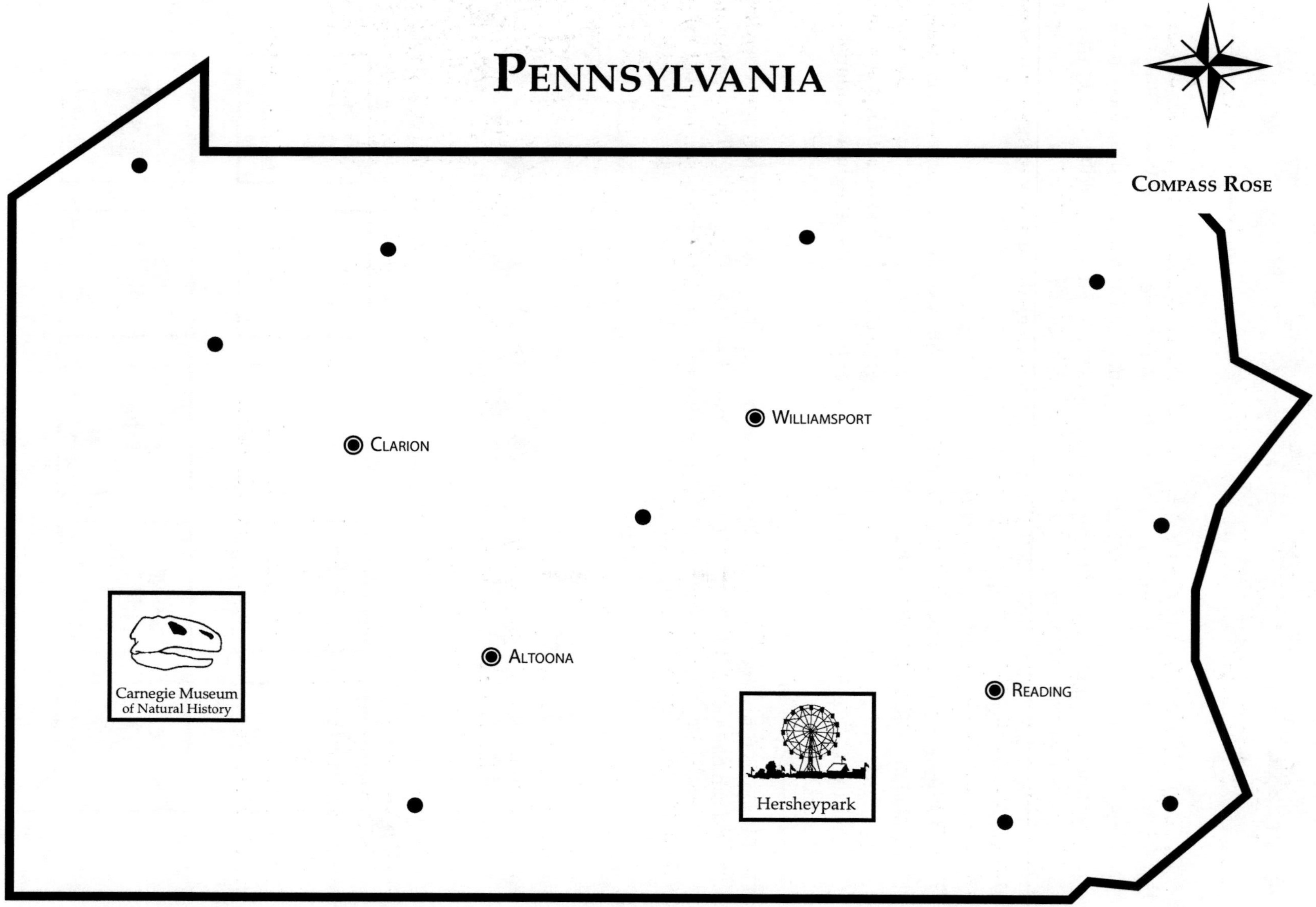

COMPASS ROSE

WILLIAMSPORT

READING

Hersheypark

CLARION

ALTOONA

Carnegie Museum
of Natural History

The Thirteen Original Colonies © 2009
splashpublications.com

★ NORTH CAROLINA ★

North Carolina, one of the five Southern colonies, is known as the Tarheel State. This nickname was chosen for North Carolina during the Revolutionary War when British soldiers marched into the Tar River. They reported that their feet were blackened with tar that had been dumped into the river.

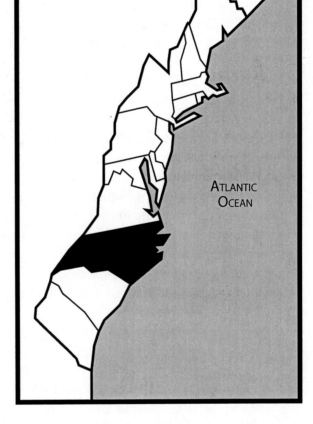

ATLANTIC OCEAN

NORTH CAROLINA'S FIRST PEOPLE

Prehistoric Native Americans once roamed through North Carolina in search of buffalo and other large game animals. Some of these animals are now **extinct**.

The **Mound Builders** arrived later and built large towns in the southern and western regions of North Carolina. At the center of each town were **ceremonial** mounds used for burying their dead. Mounds were also used as platforms for important buildings within the town.

In the 1500s, the first European explorers arrived in North Carolina. There were about 30,000 Native Americans living in the region at that time.

Two of the most powerful tribes in North Carolina were the Cherokee and the Tuscarora (tus•kuh•ROAR•uh). The Cherokee lived in the Appalachian (ap•uh•LAY•shun) Mountains. The Tuscarora people lived in villages along the rivers of North Carolina.

SIR WALTER RALEIGH

Walter Raleigh was an English soldier, explorer, writer, and businessman. As a child, Walter was well educated. He entered college at the age of 16, but only stayed one year. He made a name for himself as a soldier, fighting for England in places like **Ireland** and **Spain**. He suffered many wounds during his days as a soldier.

In 1581, at the age of 30, Raleigh met Queen Elizabeth, the ruler of England. In honor of his **military** service, Queen Elizabeth gave Raleigh 12,000 acres of land in Ireland. Raleigh used his land in Ireland to plant the country's first crops of potatoes.

ROANOKE (ROW•AN•OKE) ISLAND

Queen Elizabeth also gave Raleigh permission to establish a colony in America. In 1585, Queen Elizabeth made Walter Raleigh a **knight**. From that day forward, he was known as Sir Walter Raleigh.

Sir Walter Raleigh spent a fortune trying to establish a colony in America. In 1585, Raleigh sent a group of 108 men to Roanoke Island, near the coast of present-day North Carolina. Many of Roanoke's first colonists became very sick. After their supplies ran out, most of the men at Roanoke Island returned to England.

SIR WALTER RALEIGH

VIRGINIA DARE

In 1587, Sir Walter Raleigh sent another group of colonists to Roanoke Island. They were led by John White. This time, the group included women and children. Eleanor Dare, John White's daughter, had a baby soon after the colonists arrived in America. Her daughter, Virginia Dare, was the first English child born in the New World.

THE LOST COLONY

John White left Roanoke and sailed back to England to get more supplies for his colony. In 1591, White traveled back to Roanoke. Everyone had disappeared. What happened to the colonists at Roanoke is still a mystery to this day. Roanoke became known as the famous "Lost Colony."

THE LAND OF CHARLES

In 1653, King Charles I granted land in North Carolina to a group of colonists from Virginia. They built North Carolina's first permanent settlement. They named the land Carolina, which means "the land of Charles."

Ten years later, King Charles II gave the entire region, known as the Carolinas, to eight of his friends. The eight men called themselves the Lords **Proprietors** (pro•PRI•eh•torz). They planned to make money by renting and selling land in the Carolinas. The Lords Proprietors established a system of government for the Carolinas known as the Fundamental Constitution. Unlike other colonies, the Lords Proprietors welcomed people of all religions in the Carolinas.

BATTLES OVER LAND

The land that the Lords Proprietors sold was already owned by several Native American groups. The Native Americans attacked the new settlements. Settlers in the northern region of the Carolinas also complained of unfair laws. As a result of these problems, the first colony in the Carolinas did not do very well.

THE POOREST COLONY

In its early days, the northern region of the Carolinas was covered with trees. Settlers in the Carolina Colony had plenty of wood for building log homes furnished with wooden tables, chairs, and beds. Corn was the main crop planted by the colonists. They ate corn bread, corn stew, and corn on the cob. Mattresses were stuffed with corn husks. Any part of the corn that couldn't be eaten or used by the colonists was fed to their animals.

TOBACCO PLANT

Carolina's first colonists quickly found that the soil in Carolina was perfect for growing tobacco plants. Tobacco could be shipped to England and the Carolina colonists could become rich.

Unfortunately, the only way to send tobacco to England was by ship. Tobacco farmers in other colonies built their plantations right on the water. Big ships sailed right up to their farms and barrels of tobacco leaves were loaded onto the ships.

The coast of Carolina, on the other hand, was blocked by **sandbars** and **reefs**. Large ships could not get close enough to the shore. Some of Carolina's tobacco farmers loaded their tobacco crops into wagons and took them over dirt roads to Virginia. Others used little boats that could dock along the shore. The boats carried small amounts of tobacco to countries like Scotland, the Netherlands, and France.

The colonists in Carolina proved they could grow the tobacco. They just couldn't make any money selling it in large amounts to other countries. In Virginia, the wealthy plantation owners bought hundreds of black slaves from Africa to plant and pick the tobacco. The colonists in Carolina didn't have the money to purchase slaves. Their tobacco farms remained small.

By the late 1690s, Carolina had become the poorest of England's thirteen original colonies. Runaway slaves, poor families from other colonies, and religious groups seeking freedom all flocked to Carolina.

Name _____

Directions: Read each question carefully. Darken the circle for the correct answer.

1 North Carolina's nickname, the Tarheel State, was chosen –

　A before the colonists came to America

　B because the Atlantic Ocean was so dark it looked like tar

　C during the Revolutionary War

　D after World War II

2 Which statement about North Carolina's first people is <u>true</u>?

　F The first European explorers arrived in North Carolina during the 1700s.

　G There weren't any powerful Native American tribes in North Carolina.

　H The Cherokee lived in the White Mountains.

　J The Mound Builders arrived in North Carolina after the prehistoric hunters.

3 Which phrase about Walter Raleigh <u>best</u> describes how talented he was?

　A ...suffered many wounds...

　B ...gave Raleigh 12,000 acres of land...

　C ...soldier, explorer, writer, and businessman...

　D ...fought for England in places like Ireland and Spain...

4 What happened to the colonists on Roanoke Island?

　F They moved to Spain.

　G They mysteriously disappeared.

　H They became successful tobacco farmers.

　J They were waiting for John White when he returned from England.

5 Who was Virginia Dare?

　A John White's granddaughter.

　B John White's niece.

　C John White's cousin.

　D John White's daughter.

6 The eight men who were given the entire region of the Carolinas called themselves the Lords Proprietors. <u>Proprietors</u> are –

　F thieves

　G owners

　H presidents

　J doctors

7 Why was North Carolina known as the poorest colony?

　A They planted too much corn.

　B They had been successful cotton farmers in Virginia.

　C The soil in North Carolina wasn't good for growing anything.

　D They had no way to ship large amounts of tobacco to other countries.

READING

Answers

1　Ⓐ Ⓑ Ⓒ Ⓓ　　5　Ⓐ Ⓑ Ⓒ Ⓓ
2　Ⓕ Ⓖ Ⓗ Ⓙ　　6　Ⓕ Ⓖ Ⓗ Ⓙ
3　Ⓐ Ⓑ Ⓒ Ⓓ　　7　Ⓐ Ⓑ Ⓒ Ⓓ
4　Ⓕ Ⓖ Ⓗ Ⓙ

✩ ✦ ✫ ✦✦ VOCABULARY QUIZ ✩ ✦ ✫ ✦✦

THE THIRTEEN ORIGINAL COLONIES
PART IV

Directions: Match the vocabulary word on the left with its definition on the right. Put the letter for the definition on the blank next to the vocabulary word it matches. Use each word and definition only once.

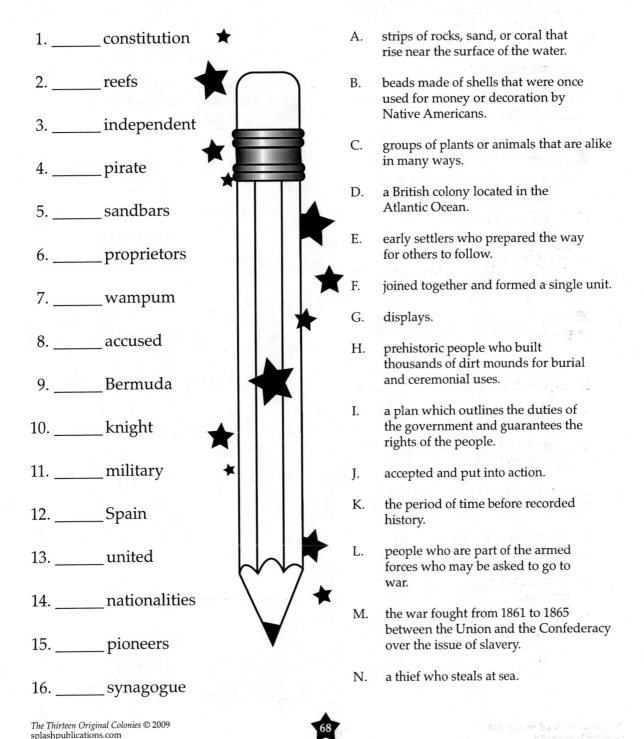

1. _____ constitution

2. _____ reefs

3. _____ independent

4. _____ pirate

5. _____ sandbars

6. _____ proprietors

7. _____ wampum

8. _____ accused

9. _____ Bermuda

10. _____ knight

11. _____ military

12. _____ Spain

13. _____ united

14. _____ nationalities

15. _____ pioneers

16. _____ synagogue

A. strips of rocks, sand, or coral that rise near the surface of the water.

B. beads made of shells that were once used for money or decoration by Native Americans.

C. groups of plants or animals that are alike in many ways.

D. a British colony located in the Atlantic Ocean.

E. early settlers who prepared the way for others to follow.

F. joined together and formed a single unit.

G. displays.

H. prehistoric people who built thousands of dirt mounds for burial and ceremonial uses.

I. a plan which outlines the duties of the government and guarantees the rights of the people.

J. accepted and put into action.

K. the period of time before recorded history.

L. people who are part of the armed forces who may be asked to go to war.

M. the war fought from 1861 to 1865 between the Union and the Confederacy over the issue of slavery.

N. a thief who steals at sea.

17. _____ Quaker

18. _____ pledged

19. _____ seized

20. _____ Commandment

21. _____ motto

22. _____ prehistoric

23. _____ extinct

24. _____ Mound Builders

25. _____ ceremonial

26. _____ Ireland

27. _____ overthrown

28. _____ elections

29. _____ adopted

30. _____ artifacts

31. _____ annual

32. _____ Civil War

33. _____ exhibits

34. _____ meadows

35. _____ species

O.   member of a religious group that believed all men were created equal, refused to serve in the Army or Navy, and would not pay taxes used to support war.

P.   a country in southwest Europe whose capital and largest city is Madrid.

Q.   objects and tools used by early humans for eating, cooking, and hunting.

R.   took by force.

S.   blamed or charged with a crime.

T.   an honor given to a man who has done something very special for Great Britain.

U.   no longer living.

V.   grassy areas used for grazing animals or for growing hay.

W.   not under the control or rule of someone else.

X.   the process of selecting leaders by voting for them.

Y.   sand that forms in a river or along the shore of the ocean because of the action of waves or currents.

Z.   an island in the northern Atlantic Ocean separated from Great Britain by the Irish Sea.

AA. a place of worship for members of the Jewish religion.

BB. a short phrase describing one's beliefs.

CC. removed from power.

DD. groups of people from different countries.

EE. promised.

FF. an event that takes place once a year.

GG. owners of a company.

HH. a type of religious or spiritual gathering.

II. one of the ten rules or laws found in the Bible.

NEW JERSEY

New Jersey, the Garden State, was one of the four Middle colonies. The state's nickname comes from New Jersey's large areas of farmland.

NEW JERSEY'S FIRST PEOPLE

The first humans in New Jersey were prehistoric people who hunted **mammoths** and other extinct animals. Historians believe that these people inhabited New Jersey thousands of years ago.

When Europeans arrived in New Jersey, they found Native Americans living in the area. These Native Americans called themselves Lenni-Lenape (len•AH•pay), meaning "original people." The Europeans called them Delaware Indians because they lived along the Delaware River.

The Delaware people built permanent settlements in New Jersey. They survived by hunting, fishing, and farming. Ashes from burned trees were used as **fertilizer** for their crops of corn, squash, and beans.

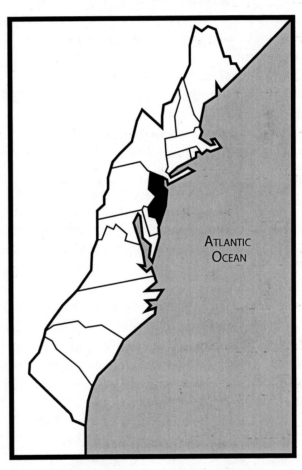

ATLANTIC OCEAN

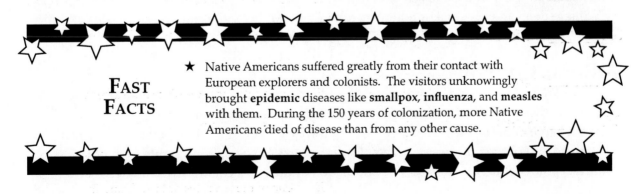

FAST FACTS

★ Native Americans suffered greatly from their contact with European explorers and colonists. The visitors unknowingly brought **epidemic** diseases like **smallpox**, **influenza**, and **measles** with them. During the 150 years of colonization, more Native Americans died of disease than from any other cause.

EUROPEAN EXPLORERS IN NEW JERSEY

In 1498, John Cabot was the first European to see New Jersey. He was an **Italian** who explored North America for England. The first European to actually visit and explore New Jersey was an explorer named Giovanni da Verrazano (vair•rot•SAH•no).

In 1524, Verrazano sailed around the tip of New Jersey and landed in New York Bay. Although Verrazano was Italian, he was exploring the land in North America for France.

In 1609, Henry Hudson, exploring for the Dutch, arrived in the New Jersey area. Nine years later, in 1618, the Dutch built the first permanent settlement in New Jersey. It was a trading post in what is now known as Jersey City.

Other Dutch settlements were established over the next 50 years, including New Netherland. Many of these settlements were destroyed during Native American attacks.

ENGLISH CONTROL OF NEW JERSEY

In 1664, King Charles II **insisted** that John Cabot had claimed New Jersey for England back in 1498. He used force and took the region for England. King Charles II gave the colony to his brother James, the Duke of York.

James gave a large part of his colony to two of his friends, Sir George Carteret (CART•uh•ret), and Lord John Berkeley. These men hoped to make money in their colony by offering colonists religious freedom and good soil to plant crops. Berkeley later sold his share of the colony to two Quakers.

In 1676, the colony was split into East Jersey and West Jersey. East Jersey was settled by the

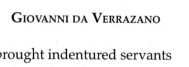

GIOVANNI DA VERRAZANO

Scottish. The Scottish built huge **estates** in East Jersey. They brought indentured servants from Scotland. They refused to sell land to anyone who wasn't Scottish. West Jersey was ruled by William Penn and his Quaker followers from England, Ireland, Scotland, and Wales. Within a short time, the populations of East and West Jersey had grown to 14,000.

A ROYAL COLONY

In 1702, Queen Anne became the ruler of England. She joined East and West Jersey back together as the single royal colony of New Jersey. Queen Anne appointed a royal governor to be in charge of the colony. The governor's job was to make sure the colonists were loyal to England and obeyed the queen's laws. Over the next 70 years, **immigrants** from other countries poured into New Jersey. The population of the royal colony swelled to 120,000.

Name _____

NEW JERSEY

Directions: Read each question carefully. Darken the circle for the correct answer.

---

1 Why is New Jersey known as the Garden State?

  A It has large areas of farmland.

  B The settlers planted huge rose gardens.

  C There are hundreds of vegetable gardens in New Jersey.

  D George Washington, the first president of the United States, thought that New Jersey had the prettiest gardens.

2 What took the lives of most Native Americans during the colonial days?

  F Wars with the colonists.

  G Accidents with guns and knives.

  H Diseases like smallpox and measles.

  J Death from old age.

3 What did the Delaware people use to fertilize their crops of corn, squash, and beans?

  A mud

  B water

  C worms

  D ashes

4 New Jersey's first people hunted <u>mammoths</u>. <u>Mammoths</u> are –

  F bears

  G whales

  H dinosaurs

  J elephants

5 Who was the first European to see New Jersey?

  A Henry Hudson

  B Queen Anne

  C George Carteret

  D John Cabot

6 Most of New Jersey's first settlements were destroyed by –

  F fires

  G floods

  H Native American attacks

  J twisters and hurricanes

7 What did King Charles II do after taking control of New Jersey?

  A He sold the land to the French.

  B He gave New Jersey to his brother.

  C He gave the land back to the Native Americans.

  D He built a castle for himself.

8 In 1676, New Jersey was split into East Jersey and West Jersey. In 1702, it was put back together as one colony. How many years passed between separating and reuniting New Jersey?

  F 21

  G 52

  H 174

  J 26

READING

Answers

1 Ⓐ Ⓑ Ⓒ Ⓓ   5 Ⓐ Ⓑ Ⓒ Ⓓ
2 Ⓕ Ⓖ Ⓗ Ⓙ   6 Ⓕ Ⓖ Ⓗ Ⓙ
3 Ⓐ Ⓑ Ⓒ Ⓓ   7 Ⓐ Ⓑ Ⓒ Ⓓ
4 Ⓕ Ⓖ Ⓗ Ⓙ   8 Ⓕ Ⓖ Ⓗ Ⓙ

A time line is a tool used to list dates and events in the order that they happened. The time line below lists important dates in New Jersey's colonial history. Notice that many of the events are missing.

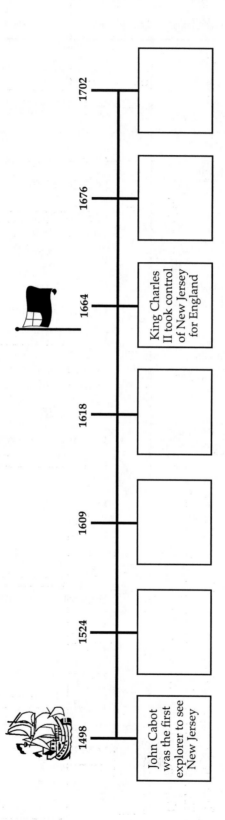

| 1498 | 1524 | 1609 | 1618 | 1664 | 1676 | 1702 |

John Cabot was the first explorer to see New Jersey

King Charles II took control of New Jersey for England

PART I

Directions: In the first part of this activity, you will use your information about New Jersey to fill in the missing events on the time line. Then, choose the picture that you think best represents each event. Color and cut out each picture before gluing it into its proper spot on the time line. Since you were not present for any of these events, this time line would be a **secondary source**.

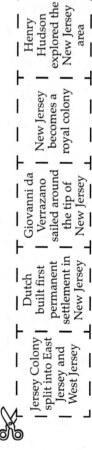

| Jersey Colony split into East Jersey and West Jersey | Dutch built first permanent settlement in New Jersey | Giovanni da Verrazano sailed around the tip of New Jersey | New Jersey becomes a royal colony | Henry Hudson explored the New Jersey area |

The Thirteen Original Colonies © 2009
splashpublications.com

PART II

Directions: In the second part of this activity, you will create a time line of someone else's life by listing the dates and events in order as they happened. Choose someone <u>outside</u> of your class: a parent, a grandparent, a friend, or another relative. Since this person will be supplying the information about his or her own life, this time line would be considered a **primary source.**

1. Use the boxes drawn to make a time line of someone else's life. Put the dates in the top boxes and the events in the bottom boxes.

2. The first date of the time line should be the person's birth. The last date should be the most recent event in his or her life.

3. Try to list only the important events. If you need more room, you may add more boxes on the back.

4. On a separate piece of paper choose one of the events from the time line and draw a picture of it.

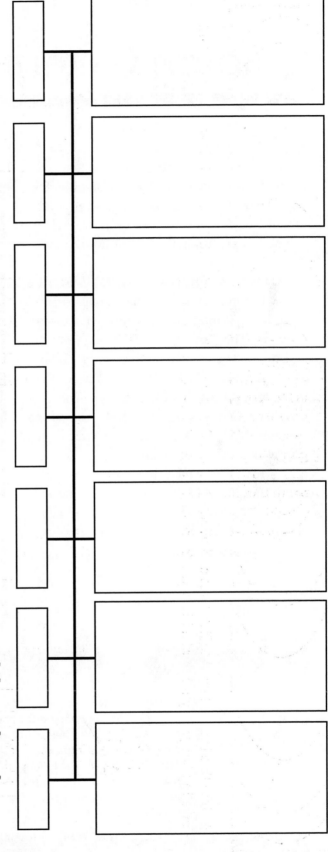

The Thirteen Original Colonies © 2009
splashpublications.com

★ SOUTH CAROLINA ★

South Carolina, the **Palmetto** State, was one of the Southern colonies. Since the late 1700s, the Palmetto has been the official **emblem** on the state flag and seal. Palmetto logs were used to build a fort that could not be destroyed by British troops during the Revolutionary War.

SOUTH CAROLINA'S FIRST PEOPLE

During South Carolina's prehistoric period, the Mound Builders built great temple mounds. These mounds have been preserved and can still be seen in South Carolina today.

Almost 30 Native American tribes lived in the area during the colonial days. The Cherokee, Catawba (kuh•TAW•buh), and the Yamasee (YAM•uh•see) were the three largest groups of Native Americans.

Today, only the Catawba remain in South Carolina on a small reservation along the Catawba River. By 1800, the rest of the Native Americans had been driven out of South Carolina by white settlers.

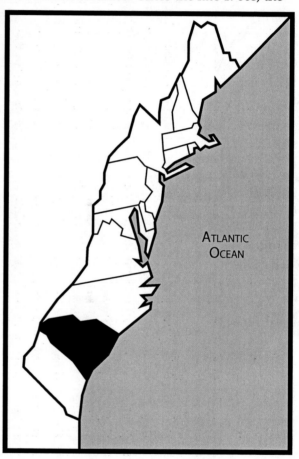

ATLANTIC OCEAN

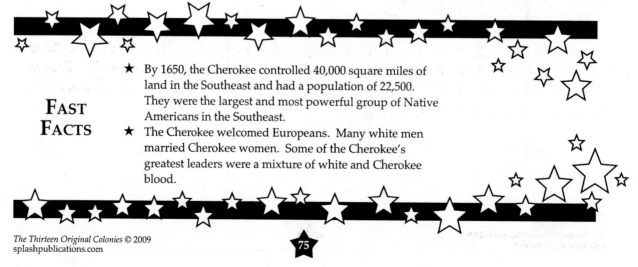

FAST FACTS

★ By 1650, the Cherokee controlled 40,000 square miles of land in the Southeast and had a population of 22,500. They were the largest and most powerful group of Native Americans in the Southeast.

★ The Cherokee welcomed Europeans. Many white men married Cherokee women. Some of the Cherokee's greatest leaders were a mixture of white and Cherokee blood.

FRANCISCO GORDILLO (GOR•DEE•YO)

In 1521, Spanish explorer Francisco Gordillo traveled to South Carolina from the Spanish-controlled islands south of Florida. These islands were discovered by Christopher Columbus. They are known today as the **West Indies**.

Gordillo wasn't interested in exploring South Carolina. He sailed to the coast of South Carolina to capture Native Americans and take them back as slaves to the West Indies.

To capture the Native Americans, Gordillo and his men played a cruel trick. Two Native Americans were invited aboard the Spanish ship. The Native Americans were treated very well and given expensive gifts. More Native Americans were invited to the ship. They were also promised gifts. About 150 Native Americans boarded the ship. Instead of gifts, they were captured and forced to sail back to the West Indies where they became slaves.

FRENCH AND SPANISH COLONIES

In 1526, Spanish ruler Lucas Vàsquez (VAZ•kez) de Ayllòn (el•YAWN) sailed from the West Indies to South Carolina. One of Gordillo's Native American captives had told Ayllòn stories about treasures in South Carolina. Ayllòn planned to start a Spanish colony in South Carolina. He arrived in South Carolina with more than 500 people and hundreds of farm animals.

Within a few months, de Ayllòn and most of his colonists died from starvation and disease. In October 1526, the few surviving settlers returned to the West Indies.

In 1562, French explorer Jean Ribaut (ree•BOH) led 150 men from France to South Carolina. Ribaut planned to build a colony where French Protestants could worship freely. They built a military fort along the southeastern coast of South Carolina.

FRANCISCO GORDILLO

In the spring, Ribaut and many of the men returned to France for more colonists and supplies. The colonists who remained failed to plant crops and nearly starved to death. After a year of waiting for Ribaut to return, the colonists built a boat and tried to sail back to France. Along the way, the men ran out of food. Several died from hunger. In order to survive, the group killed and ate one of its own men.

THE CHARLES TOWN COLONY

Over the next 100 years, Spanish and French colonists tried to start other colonies in South Carolina. All of these attempts failed. Native American conflicts, starvation, and disease kept the Spanish and French colonists from building South Carolina's first permanent settlement.

In 1663, King Charles II of England granted land known as the Carolinas to eight of his friends. The eight men called themselves the Lords Proprietors (pro•PRI•eh•torz). You have already read that these men planned to make money by renting and selling land in the Carolinas.

In 1670, the first 100 colonists sailed from England to the southern region of the Carolinas. They founded the first permanent settlement in present-day South Carolina. In honor of King Charles II, the colony was named Charles Town. The name was later changed to Charleston.

The colonists of Charles Town were not very good farmers. At first, they traded with the Native Americans for corn and other supplies. Later, the colonists learned to plant and grow rice. During the 1700s, rice and indigo became the leading crops in Charles Town and other new settlements. These crops brought a lot of wealth to the southern part of the Carolinas. Plantation owners bought slaves from Africa to help them grow the rice and indigo. By 1708, there were more black slaves than white settlers living in the southern region of the Carolinas. The colonists bought more slaves than they needed and traded or sold them to other colonies.

SEPARATING THE CAROLINAS

Maintaining peace in the Carolinas was difficult during the early days. The Native Americans, especially the Yamasee tribe, made life difficult for the settlers. Constant threats by the Spanish in Florida also destroyed the peace in the Carolinas. The settlers were also unhappy with the government in the Carolinas. In 1729, the settlers asked King George II to separate the southern region from the rest of the Carolinas. He agreed and divided the Carolinas into North Carolina and South Carolina. Both regions became royal colonies. This meant that they were controlled by Great Britain.

South Carolina became very wealthy under Great Britain's rule. Like the other twelve colonies, it was anxious to break away from Great Britain and become independent. Great Britain received a lot of money from its colonies in America. It was not interested in allowing the colonists to be independent. This power struggle between Great Britain and the English colonists in America led to the Revolutionary War.

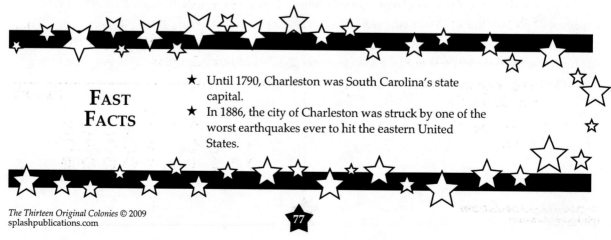

FAST FACTS

★ Until 1790, Charleston was South Carolina's state capital.
★ In 1886, the city of Charleston was struck by one of the worst earthquakes ever to hit the eastern United States.

Name _____

Directions: Read each question carefully. Darken the circle for the correct answer.

1 South Carolina is known as the <u>Palmetto</u> State. A <u>palmetto</u> is a type of –

   A candy

   B flower

   C vegetable

   D tree

2 Which Native American group still lives in South Carolina today?

   F Cherokee

   G Yamasee

   H Catawba

   J Mound Builders

3 Why did Francisco Gordillo sail to the coast of South Carolina?

   A He wanted to pick up a load of tobacco.

   B He wanted to build a colony along South Carolina's coast.

   C He planned to capture Native Americans and take them back as slaves.

   D He was interested in exploring South Carolina.

4 Which statement about South Carolina's first Spanish colony is <u>false</u>?

   F The colony was established by Lucas Vásquez de Ayllón.

   G Most of the colonists died of starvation and disease.

   H The colony was started with more than 500 people.

   J Some of the colonists moved to Canada.

5 How was South Carolina's first French colony a lot like the English colonies you have been reading about?

   A The colonists were searching for religious freedom.

   B They planted crops.

   C They brought black slaves with them to work on their huge plantations.

   D They paid the Native Americans for their land.

6 After reading about the colony in Charles Town, you learn that –

   F the colonists were excellent farmers

   G they were the only southern colony to refuse the help of black slaves

   H plantation owners in Charles Town grew rice and indigo

   J Charles Town was named in honor of the Duke of Charles

7 All of the following statements about the early days of the Carolinas are true <u>except</u> –

   A the Spanish in Florida made peace in the Carolinas difficult

   B the Native Americans welcomed the colonists in the Carolinas

   C the settlers in the Carolinas were not happy with the government's leadership

   D in 1729, King George II separated the Carolinas into North Carolina and South Carolina

Answers   **READING**

1 Ⓐ Ⓑ Ⓒ Ⓓ   5 Ⓐ Ⓑ Ⓒ Ⓓ

2 Ⓕ Ⓖ Ⓗ Ⓙ   6 Ⓕ Ⓖ Ⓗ Ⓙ

3 Ⓐ Ⓑ Ⓒ Ⓓ   7 Ⓐ Ⓑ Ⓒ Ⓓ

4 Ⓕ Ⓖ Ⓗ Ⓙ

Name _____

FAMOUS COLONISTS
K·W·L·H CHART

Throughout American History, many people have helped shape our nation. In this activity you will use **primary** and **secondary sources** to research one of the colonists you have learned about so far. Choose from John Smith, George Calvert, Thomas Hooker, William Penn, and Sir Walter Raleigh. Answer the questions below to get you started. Then use the charts on the next two pages to record your information.

1   **Which colonist did you choose?** _____

2   **Why did this colonist come to America?** _____

3   **Describe one challenge that this colonist faced in the New World.** _____
_____
_____

4   **How did this colonist solve his problems?** _____
_____
_____

DIRECTIONS:

1. Use the "What I Know" column of the charts on the next two pages to list facts that you already know about the colonist.

2. Use the "What I Want to Know" column of the charts to list five questions that you have about the colonist.

3. Use books, encyclopedias, the Internet, and other sources to research and answer your questions. Write your answers in the "What I Learned" column of the charts.

4. List the book titles, encyclopedias, and website addresses that you used to find your information in the "How I Found Out" column of the charts.

5. Put a "P" next to the **primary sources** and an "S" next to the **secondary sources** that you used to find your information.

WHAT I KNOW	WHAT I WANT TO KNOW	WHAT I LEARNED	HOW I FOUND OUT	P / S

The Thirteen Original Colonies © 2009
splashpublications.com

P/S			
HOW I FOUND OUT			
WHAT I LEARNED			
WHAT I WANT TO KNOW			
WHAT I KNOW			

☆ ✦✶ ★✶ FAMOUS COLONISTS ☆ ✦ ☆ ★✶

LET'S TALK ABOUT IT

Now that you have finished your research and filled in the K•W•L•H Chart for one of the colonists, let's talk about what you have learned. Read the questions below and write your answers on the lines provided. Attach a separate piece of paper if you need more room. Be ready to discuss some of your answers.

1 **Based on your research, what is the most important <u>new</u> detail that you learned about the colonist you chose?**

_____

_____

2 **Did your research change the way you thought about this colonist? Explain your answer.**

_____

_____

3 **Describe one important contribution that this colonist made to the New World.**

_____

_____

_____

4 **Is this contribution still important to us today? Explain your answer.**

_____

_____

_____

GEORGIA

Georgia, one of the five Southern colonies, is known as the Peach State. Georgia's peach growers are known for producing high quality peaches. In 1995, the peach became Georgia's official state fruit.

A DEBTOR'S COLONY

Before European settlers arrived, Georgia was home to Native Americans of the peaceful Cherokee and Creek tribes. In 1539, Spanish explorer Hernando de Soto passed through Georgia looking for gold. As a result of de Soto's travels, Georgia was claimed by Spain.

England didn't care about Spain's claim to Georgia. In 1732, King George II granted a charter to a group of wealthy Englishmen headed by James E. Oglethorpe.

The plan was to start a colony for people in the other twelve colonies who were poor, in debt, or unable to find a job. King George II hoped that the colonists in Georgia would be able to keep out the Spaniards in Florida and the French in Louisiana. Oglethorpe also wanted to offer religious freedom to Protestants from Germany and Austria.

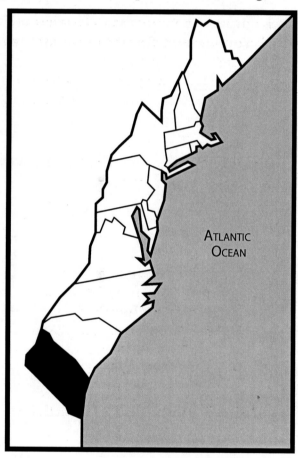

ATLANTIC OCEAN

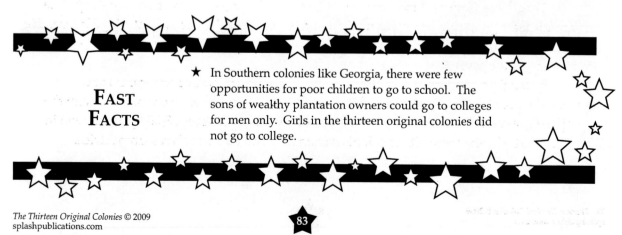

FAST FACTS

★ In Southern colonies like Georgia, there were few opportunities for poor children to go to school. The sons of wealthy plantation owners could go to colleges for men only. Girls in the thirteen original colonies did not go to college.

RAISING SILKWORMS IN GEORGIA

Georgia would be a place for colonists to earn money by raising silkworms and planting crops of wine grapes. The profits from selling these items would be used to pay the settlers' debts.

In 1733, James Oglethorpe arrived in Georgia with about 120 followers. He settled in Savannah and named his colony Georgia, in honor of King George II. This was the last of the thirteen original colonies established by England.

Each settler was given 50 acres of land for raising their wine grapes and silkworms. The colonists were not allowed to buy slaves to help work their small farms.

Unfortunately, many of the colonists got sick with **malaria**. They found it impossible to keep up with the large farms worked by slaves in nearby South Carolina. The colonists also discovered that silkworms and wine grapes did not grow well in Georgia's soil. Many of the colonists left.

JAMES OGLETHORPE

DEFENDING GEORGIA

James Oglethorpe was told that Spain was planning to take over Georgia.

In 1734, Oglethorpe went back to England. He brought back more colonists and soldiers. In 1736, he built Fort Frederica to protect his colony. In 1742, Spaniards from Florida attacked Georgia. James Oglethorpe was ready for them. Oglethorpe's soldiers defeated the Spaniards and **retained** Georgia for England.

GEORGIA BECOMES A ROYAL COLONY

In 1752, King George II took control of Georgia. Georgia became a royal colony. The king appointed a governor, a royal council, and allowed the colonists to elect a **legislature**. He gave the settlers more land and permitted them to buy slaves. King George II let the colonists plant whatever they wanted.

The colonists developed friendly relationships with the Native Americans and established a profitable fur trade with them. Rice, indigo, and wheat were planted with the help of black slaves. Cattle and hogs were raised. By the 1760s, about 3,000 people lived in Georgia. Most of them were either colonists from England or black slaves from Africa.

Name _____

Directions: Read each question carefully. Darken the circle for the correct answer.

1   In what year did the peach become Georgia's official state fruit?

　　A 1897

　　B 1980

　　C 1995

　　D 1732

2   Which country claimed Georgia <u>first</u>?

　　F Spain

　　G France

　　H Germany

　　J England

3   What was King George II's reason for establishing a colony in Georgia?

　　A He planned to allow people from all countries to live in Georgia.

　　B He wanted to find a place where Native Americans could live in peace.

　　C He was interested in growing orchards of peaches and apples to send back to England.

　　D The colony in Georgia would be for people in the other twelve colonies who were poor, in debt, or unable to find a job.

4   What can you learn by studying Georgia's map of the thirteen original colonies?

　　F Georgia is the southernmost of the thirteen colonies.

　　G Georgia is not connected to the other colonies.

　　H Georgia is the northernmost of the thirteen colonies.

　　J Georgia is in the middle of the thirteen colonies.

5   Why was it difficult for Georgia's colonists to raise silkworms and wine grapes?

　　A Many of the colonists became sick with malaria.

　　B Silkworms and wine grapes did not grow well in Georgia's soil.

　　C The colonists were not permitted to buy slaves to help work on their farms.

　　D All of the above.

6   Why did James Oglethorpe build Fort Frederica?

　　F He wanted to build a place where the colonists and Native Americans could trade beaver furs.

　　G Fort Frederica was built as a church.

　　H The fort was built to protect the Georgia colony.

　　J Oglethorpe planned to sell wine and silk from Fort Frederica.

7   When Georgia became a royal colony, what changed?

　　A King George II took all of the land away from the colonists.

　　B The colonists were permitted to plant whatever they wanted and buy slaves.

　　C The Native Americans were no longer interested in trading with the colonists.

　　D James Oglethorpe took complete control of Georgia.

READING

Answers

1 Ⓐ Ⓑ Ⓒ Ⓓ   5 Ⓐ Ⓑ Ⓒ Ⓓ
2 Ⓕ Ⓖ Ⓗ Ⓙ   6 Ⓕ Ⓖ Ⓗ Ⓙ
3 Ⓐ Ⓑ Ⓒ Ⓓ   7 Ⓐ Ⓑ Ⓒ Ⓓ
4 Ⓕ Ⓖ Ⓗ Ⓙ

THIRTEEN ORIGINAL COLONIES
★ QUIZ ★

The thirteen original colonies were Connecticut, Delaware, Georgia, Maryland, Massachusetts, New Hampshire, New Jersey, New York, North Carolina, Pennsylvania, Rhode Island, South Carolina, and Virginia.

Label each of the thirteen original colonies on the map below. Color the New England colonies blue, the Middle colonies green, and the Southern colonies red.

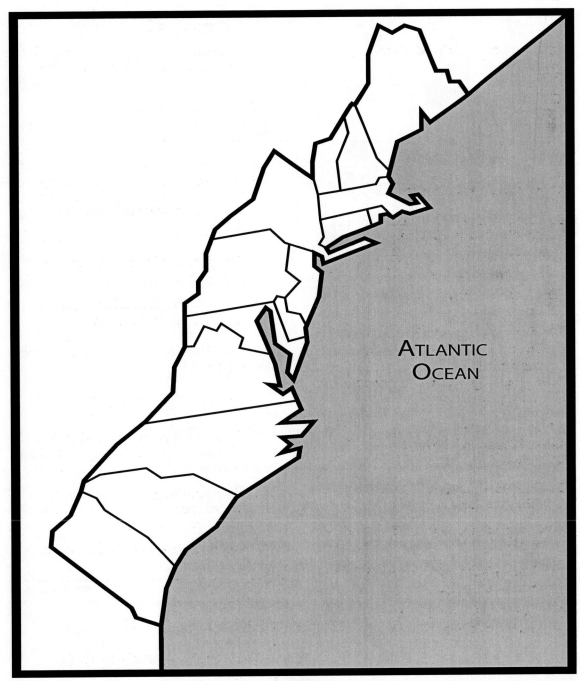

ATLANTIC
OCEAN

Name _____

Directions: Match the vocabulary word on the left with its definition on the right. Put the letter for the definition on the blank next to the vocabulary word it matches. Use each word and definition only once.

1. _____ mammoths

2. _____ legislature

3. _____ palmetto

4. _____ fertilizer

5. _____ retained

6. _____ epidemic

7. _____ emblem

8. _____ malaria

9. _____ smallpox

10. _____ estates

11. _____ military

12. _____ West Indies

13. _____ immigrants

14. _____ Italian

15. _____ measles

16. _____ insisted

A.   material added to the soil to make crops grow better.

B.   an object that represents something.

C.   a group of people with the power to make laws.

D.   people who permanently settle in another country.

E.   a person from Italy, a country in southern Europe that sticks out into the Mediterranean Sea.

F.   an illness that causes fever and red spots all over the skin.

G.   large country houses on big pieces of land.

H.   a palm tree with leaves shaped like fans.

I.   a disease that spreads quickly and affects many people at the same time.

J.   a disease that can be easily spread to other people, causing fever, weakness, and puss filled bumps that usually leave scars.

K.   demanded.

L.   a chain of about 1,000 islands in the Caribbean Sea that stretches from the southern tip of Florida to the northeastern corner of South America.

M.   large, hairy, extinct elephants with tusks that curved upward.

N.   a disease caused by mosquitoes that spreads to other humans and results in chills and fever.

O.   people who are part of the armed forces who may be asked to go to war.

P.   kept control of.

GLOSSARY

ac•cused blamed or charged with a crime.

ad•mired thought highly of.

a•dop•ted accepted and put into action.

A•fri•ca second largest continent in the world.

al•lies groups of people who come together to help one another in times of trouble.

an•nu•al an event that takes place once a year.

ap•point•ed chosen or selected.

ar•ti•facts objects and tools used by early humans for eating, cooking, and hunting.

A•sia the world's largest continent with more than half of the Earth's population.

as•sault a violent attack.

au•to•bi•og•ra•phy the story of your life written by you.

bay a body of water surrounded by land that opens to the sea.

Ber•mu•da a British colony located in the Atlantic Ocean.

bi•og•ra•phies stories of a person's life written by someone else.

bound•a•ries dividing lines.

cap•tives prisoners who have been taken by force without permission.

Cath•o•lics members of a Christian church who trace their history back to the twelve apostles.

cer•e•mo•ni•al a type of religious or spiritual gathering.

char•ter a contract which gives one group power over another.

Chris•tians people who belong to a religion based on the life and teachings of Jesus Christ.

Church of En•gland the official church in England.

Civ•il War the war fought from 1861 to 1865 between the Union and the Confederacy over the issue of slavery.

cli•mate the average weather conditions of an area over a period of years.

coast an area of land that borders water.

col•o•nies groups of people who are ruled by another country.

Com•mand•ment one of the ten rules or laws found in the Bible.

con•fed•er•a•cy a group of people with common goals.

con•flict a struggle or disagreement.

con•sti•tu•tion a plan which outlines the duties of the government and guarantees the rights of the people.

coun•cil a group of people chosen to make laws or give advice.

cul•ti•vate to prepare the soil for growing crops.

debt money that is owed to someone else.

de•feat•ed won victory over.

in•sis•ted demanded.

de•struc•tive causing damage.

de•ter•mi•na•tion making a decision and sticking to it, no matter how difficult.

do•min•ion a territory with one ruler.

Dutch people who are from the Netherlands, a country of northwest Europe on the North Sea.

e•lec•tions the process of selecting leaders by voting for them.

em•blem an object that represents something.

em•pire a group of territories or peoples under one ruler.

en•cour•aged gave support, courage, or hope to someone.

En•gland a region located on the southern part of the island of Great Britain.

ep•i•dem•ic a disease that spreads quickly and affects many people at the same time.

es•tates large country houses on big pieces of land.

Eu•ro•pe•an a person who comes from the continent of Europe.

ex•hib•its displays.

ex•pand•ing growing larger.

ex•pe•di•tion a journey for the purpose of exploring.

ex•tinct no longer living.

fer•tile rich soil that produces a large number of crops.

fer•ti•liz•er material added to the soil to make crops grow better.

for•ma•tions arrangements of something.

found•ed started or established.

French a person from France, a country in western Europe.

fun•gus a disease that destroys plants.

gov•er•nor a person who is in charge of an area or group.

gran•ite a hard rock formed millions of years ago that contains crystals.

Great Lakes five large lakes located in North America at the border between Canada and the United States. The names of the lakes are Superior, Michigan, Huron, Erie, and Ontario.

Green•land the world's largest island. Located northeast of North America.

grist•mills mills for grinding grain into flour.

har•bors sheltered areas of water deep enough to provide ships a place to anchor.

har•vest•ed picked crops.

his•to•ri•ans people who study history.

im•mi•grants people who permanently settle in another country.

in•ci•sor one of four front cutting teeth in the upper or lower jaw.

in•den•tured ser•vants people who agreed to work for someone else in return for payment of travel expenses to America.

in•de•pen•dent not under the control or rule of someone else.

in•di•go a plant which produces a blue dye.

in•flu•en•za an illness that affects the lungs and causes fever, chills, muscular pain, and headaches.

in•hab•it•ed lived or settled in a place.

in•sis•ted demanded.

in•te•ri•or the inside of something.

Ire•land an island in the northern Atlantic Ocean separated from Great Britain by the Irish Sea.

I•tal•ian a person from Italy, a country in southern Europe that sticks out into the Mediterranean Sea.

keel•boats shallow covered river boats that are usually rowed or towed and used for carrying supplies.

kid•napped took someone without permission.

knight an honor given to a man who has done something very special for Great Britain.

leg•is•la•ture a group of people with the power to make laws.

live•stock animals raised on a farm to eat or sell for profit.

long•house long dwelling where many Native American families live at the same time.

loy•al faithful.

ma•lar•i•a a disease caused by mosquitoes that spreads to other humans and results in chills and fever.

mam•moths large, hairy, extinct elephants with tusks that curved upward.

mead•ows grassy areas used for grazing animals or for growing hay.

mea•sles an illness that causes fever and red spots all over the skin.

mer•chants buyers and sellers whose goal is to make money.

mil•i•tar•y people who are part of the armed forces who may be asked to go to war.

mi•li•tia a group of men having some military training who are called upon only in emergencies.

mot•to a short phrase describing one's beliefs.

Mound Build•ers prehistoric people who built thousands of dirt mounds for burial and ceremonial uses.

na•tion•al•i•ties groups of people from different countries.

New World a term once used to describe the continents of North America and South America.

North A•mer•i•ca one of seven continents in the world. Bounded by Alaska on the northwest, Greenland on the northeast, Florida on the southeast, and Mexico on the southwest.

North Pole the northernmost point on the Earth.

of•fi•cial proper or correct.

or•chards groups of fruit or nut trees.

o•ver•thrown removed from power.

pal•met•to a palm tree with leaves shaped like fans.

Pil•grims the English colonists who founded the first permanent settlement in the New England colony of Plymouth in 1620.

pi•o•neers early settlers who prepared the way for others to follow.

pi•rate a thief who steals at sea.

plan•ta•tions very large farms in the South where crops of cotton and tobacco were grown and slave labor was usually used.

pledged promised.

pre•his•tor•ic the period of time before recorded history.

pre•served protected from injury or ruin so more could be learned.

pro•duc•tion the act of making something.

pro•fit money made after all expenses have been paid.

pro•pri•e•tors owners of a company.

pros•per to have success or wealth.

Prot•es•tants members of a Christian church other than the Roman Catholic Church.

prov•ince a part of a country having a government of its own.

Pu•ri•tan a person from England who traveled to America in the 1600s and 1700s in search of religious freedom.

Qua•ker member of a religious group that believed all men were created equal, refused to serve in the Army or Navy, and would not pay taxes used to support war.

quar•rel•ing arguing and fighting.

raid•ed suddenly attacked.

re•bel•lion acting out against authority.

reefs strips of rocks, sand, or coral that rise near the surface of the water.

rep•re•sen•ta•tives people chosen to speak or act for an entire group.

re•sourc•es things found in nature that are valuable to humans.

re•tained kept control of.

re•volt•ed fought against rules and laws felt to be unfair.

Rev•o•lu•tion•ar•y War battle for independence between the English colonists in America and Great Britain.

ro•dent small mammal with large front teeth used for gnawing or nibbling.

sand•bars sand that forms in a river or along the shore of the ocean because of the action of waves or currents.

saw•mills businesses with big machines that saw wood into planks and boards.

scalps the tops of human heads that are usually covered with hair.

Scot•land one of the four countries that make up Great Britain and Northern Ireland; famous for bagpipes and plaid skirts known as kilts.

sea•coast land that borders the sea.

sea•port a sheltered area where ships can load and unload supplies.

seized took by force.

shore•line the edge of a body of water.

small•pox a disease that can be easily spread to other people, causing fever, weakness, and puss filled bumps that usually leave scars.

Spain a country in southwest Europe whose capital and largest city is Madrid.

spe•cies groups of plants or animals that are alike in many ways.

stat•ute a rule or law.

strait a narrow strip of sea between two pieces of land.

syn•a•gogue a place of worship for members of the Jewish religion.

threat•ened made plans to harm someone.

tram•pled walked heavily on something and crushed or destroyed it.

trea•ty a formal agreement.

tur•moil constant confusion and disorder.

u•nit•ed joined together and formed a single unit.

voy•ag•es journeys that are usually made by water.

wam•pum beads made of shells that were once used for money or decoration by Native Americans.

West In•dies a chain of about 1,000 islands in the Caribbean Sea that stretches from the southern tip of Florida to the northeastern corner of South America.

wig•wam a Native American home made of poles and covered with bark, mats, or animal skins.

ANSWERS

ANSWERS TO COMPREHENSION QUESTIONS

VIRGINIA

1. B
2. J
3. C
4. G
5. A
6. G
7. C

MASSACHUSETTS

1. A
2. H
3. B
4. H
5. D
6. F
7. C

NEW HAMPSHIRE

1. C
2. J
3. A
4. G
5. C
6. F
7. C
8. F

NEW YORK

1. B
2. G
3. A
4. J
5. B
6. J

MARYLAND

1. C
2. J
3. A
4. H
5. B
6. G

CONNECTICUT

1. D
2. J
3. C
4. F
5. B
6. J
7. B

RHODE ISLAND

1. C
2. J
3. A
4. J
5. C
6. F
7. C

DELAWARE

1. A
2. G
3. D
4. H
5. B
6. G
7. C

PENNSYLVANIA

1. B
2. H
3. D
4. H
5. A
6. J
7. A

NORTH CAROLINA

1. C
2. J
3. C
4. G
5. A
6. G
7. D

NEW JERSEY

1. A
2. H
3. D
4. J
5. D
6. H
7. B
8. J

SOUTH CAROLINA

1. D
2. H
3. C
4. J
5. A
6. H
7. B

GEORGIA

1. C
2. F
3. D
4. F
5. D
6. H
7. B

ANSWERS TO VOCABULARY QUIZZES

PART I	PART II	PART III	PART IV	PART V
1. FF	1. G	1. CC	1. I	1. M
2. L	2. Q	2. B	2. A	2. C
3. Y	3. FF	3. K	3. W	3. H
4. A	4. A	4. Q	4. N	4. A
5. Q	5. S	5. G	5. Y	5. P
6. I	6. K	6. U	6. GG	6. I
7. EE	7. U	7. AA	7. B	7. B
8. U	8. AA	8. A	8. S	8. N
9. M	9. O	9. N	9. D	9. J
10. AA	10. C	10. D	10. T	10. G
11. B	11. V	11. O	11. L	11. O
12. V	12. R	12. T	12. P	12. L
13. J	13. I	13. J	13. F	13. D
14. O	14. T	14. M	14. DD	14. E
15. F	15. Z	15. W	15. E	15. F
16. N	16. X	16. E	16. AA	16. K
17. W	17. N	17. V	17. O	
18. C	18. CC	18. H	18. EE	
19. DD	19. E	19. P	19. R	
20. E	20. EE	20. C	20. II	
21. CC	21. GG	21. R	21. BB	
22. G	22. B	22. BB	22. K	
23. P	23. BB	23. S	23. U	
24. D	24. J	24. Y	24. H	
25. Z	25. DD	25. F	25. HH	
26. K	26. D	26. X	26. Z	
27. BB	27. W	27. L	27. CC	
28. R	28. F	28. Z	28. X	
29. X	29. L	29. I	29. J	
30. S	30. M		30. Q	
31. T	31. H		31. FF	
32. GG	32. P		32. M	
33. H	33. Y		33. G	
			34. V	
			35. C	

The Thirteen Original Colonies © 2009
splashpublications.com

ANSWERS TO CONSIDER THE SOURCE

1. S
2. S
3. P
4. P
5. P
6. S
7. P

ANSWERS TO STUDY GUIDE AND QUIZ

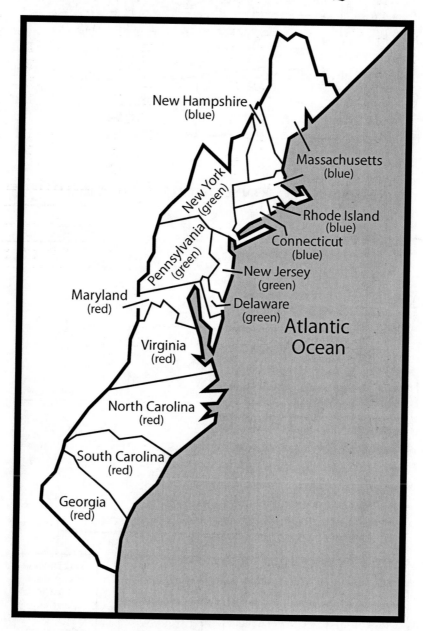

New Hampshire
(blue)

Massachusetts
(blue)

New York
(green)

Rhode Island
(blue)

Connecticut
(blue)

Pennsylvania
(green)

New Jersey
(green)

Maryland
(red)

Delaware
(green)

Atlantic
Ocean

Virginia
(red)

North Carolina
(red)

South Carolina
(red)

Georgia
(red)

ANSWERS TO MASSACHUSETTS GRID MATH

ANSWERS TO CONNECTICUT TIME TRAVEL

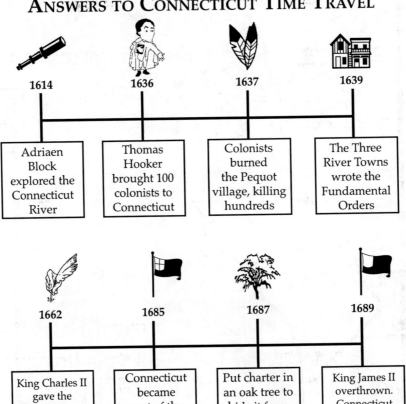

1614
Adriaen Block explored the Connecticut River

1636
Thomas Hooker brought 100 colonists to Connecticut

1637
Colonists burned the Pequot village, killing hundreds

1639
The Three River Towns wrote the Fundamental Orders

1662
King Charles II gave the Connecticut Colony its own charter

1685
Connecticut became part of the Dominion of New England

1687
Put charter in an oak tree to hide it from Governor Andros

1689
King James II overthrown. Connecticut became separate colony

FIND THE FIB GRADING CHART

CRITERIA	POINTS POSSIBLE	POINTS EARNED
Fifteen True Facts	60 (4 pts. each)	
Five False Facts	20 (4 pts. each)	
Creativity of Design	10	
Neatness	5	
Answer Sheet	5	
TOTAL	100	

ANSWERS TO PENNSYLVANIA MAPPING

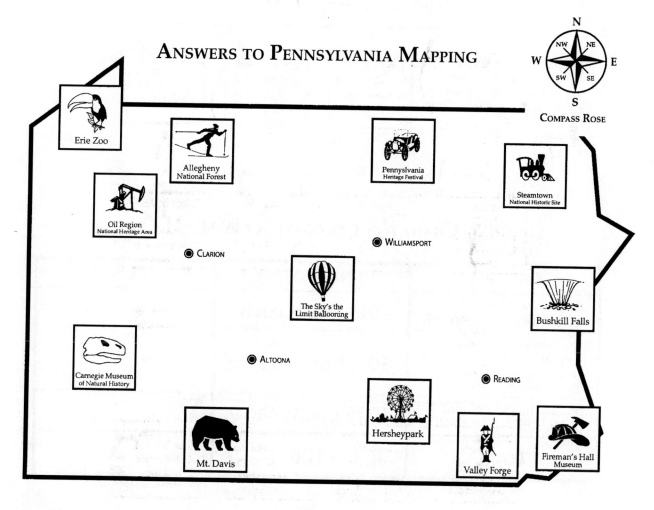

ANSWERS TO NEW JERSEY TIME TRAVEL

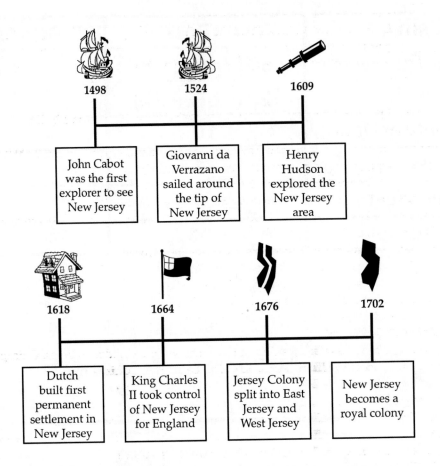

1498 — John Cabot was the first explorer to see New Jersey

1524 — Giovanni da Verrazano sailed around the tip of New Jersey

1609 — Henry Hudson explored the New Jersey area

1618 — Dutch built first permanent settlement in New Jersey

1664 — King Charles II took control of New Jersey for England

1676 — Jersey Colony split into East Jersey and West Jersey

1702 — New Jersey becomes a royal colony

GRADING CHART FOR COLONIST K • W • L • H CHART

CRITERIA	POINTS POSSIBLE	POINTS EARNED
Answering 4 Questions Before Beginning Research	**20** (5 points each)	
Completing 5 Sections of K-W-L-H Chart (What I **Know**, What I **Want** to Know, What I **Learned**, **How** I Found Out)	**60** (12 points each)	
Answering 4 Questions After Finishing Research	**20** (5 points each)	
TOTAL	**100**	

The Thirteen Original Colonies © 2009
splashpublications.com

BIBLIOGRAPHY

American Heritage Dictionary of the English Language, Fourth Edition, Houghton Mifflin, Massachusetts, 2000.

Bartleby: 'American Heritage Dictionary of the English Language: Fourth Edition' 2000 [Online] Available <http://www.bartleby.com> (August 23, 2007)

Blashfield, Jean (2000), *Delaware: America the Beautiful,* Children's Press, New York

Blashfield, Jean (1999), *Virginia: America the Beautiful,* Children's Press, New York

Baranzini, Marlene and Bovert, Howard (1995), *US Kids History Book of the New American Nation,* Yolla Bolly Press, California

Carter, Alden R. (1988), *Birth of the Republic,* Frank Watts, New York

Davis, Kenneth (2001), *Don't Know Much about the 50 States!,* Harper Collins, USA

Fradin, Dennis (1990), *The Connecticut Colony,* Children's Press, Chicago

Fradin, Dennis (1992), *The Delaware Colony,* Children's Press, Chicago

Fradin, Dennis (1990), *The Georgia Colony,* Children's Press, Chicago

Fradin, Dennis (1990), *The Maryland Colony,* Children's Press, Chicago

Fradin, Dennis (1987), *The Massachusetts Colony,* Regensteiner and Children's Press, Chicago

Fradin, Dennis (1988), *The New Hampshire Colony,* Children's Press, Chicago

Fradin, Dennis (1991), *The New Jersey Colony,* Children's Press, Chicago

Fradin, Dennis (1988), *The New York Colony,* Children's Press, Chicago

Fradin, Dennis (1991), *The North Carolina Colony,* Children's Press, Chicago

Fradin, Dennis (1988), *The Pennsylvania Colony,* Regensteiner and Children's Press, Chicago

Fradin, Dennis (1989), *The Rhode Island Colony,* Children's Press, Chicago

Fradin, Dennis (1995), *Rhode Island: From Sea to Shining Sea,* Children's Press, Chicago

Fradin, Dennis and Judith (1992), *The South Carolina Colony,* Children's Press, Connecticut

Headley, Amy and Smith, Victoria. (2003), *Do American History!* Splash! Publications, Arizona

Hintz, Martin and Stephen (1998), *North Carolina: America the Beautiful,* Children's Press, New York

Isaacs, Sally Senzell (1998), *America in the Time of Pocahontas,* Heinemann Library, Illinois

Internet School Library Media Center: 'Colonial America 1600-1775 K12 Resources' 2003 [Online] Available <http://falcon.jmu.edu/~ramseyil/colonial.htm#A> (March 10, 2008)

Kent, Deborah (1987), *New Jersey: America the Beautiful,* Regensteiner and Children's Press, Chicago

Krull, Kathleen (1997), *Wish You Were Here: Emily's Guide to the 50 States,* Bantam Doubleday, New York

Lee, John and Susan (1974), *George Washington,* Regensteiner, Chicago

Lexico Publishing Group: 'Dictionary.com' 2004 [Online] Available <http://dictionary.reference.com/> (September 1, 2008)

Masters, Nancy Robinson (1999), *Georgia: America the Beautiful,* Children's Press, New York

McNair, Sylvia (1999), *Connecticut: America the Beautiful,* Children's Press, New York

Stein, Conrad (1999), *South Carolina: America the Beautiful,* Children's Press, New York

Steins, Richard (2000), *Exploration and Settlement,* Steck-Vaughn, Texas

Webster's Revised Unabridged Dictionary, MICRA, New Jersey, 1998.

Woods, Mario (1997), *The World of Native Americans,* Peter Bedrick Books, New York